MW00389064

Finding a Place in the World

Ann Girson Schorr

DEDICATION

This memoir is dedicated to the memory of
my parents, Benjamin and Dora Girson,
whose vision made it possible for me to find
my place in the world.

Benjamin and Dora Girson

ACKNOWLEDGMENTS

To the many members of my extended family who provided information, confirmed events and chronology, read and commented on drafts; and

To the many friends who encouraged me before and during the long process of writing; and

To my children, Jessica, Kenneth and Wendy, who made the publication of this memoir possible.

CONTENTS

FOREWORD

When we were children, our mother occasionally talked to us of her childhood in Argentina. We knew about Tuviana, her horse. We knew of the gaucho named Don Francisco, who lived at her farm, told her stories, and was like a beloved godfather to her and her sisters. We were the only family in the neighborhood that sometimes had dulce de leche, a sweet caramel spread, with a flavor that had not yet found its way into American ice creams. And she sang us "Arroz con Leche."

Her childhood in distant lands where she spoke other languages (not one, but three: first Russian, then Yiddish and Spanish) seemed exotic, remote, and mysterious. Choice details like riding a horse to school added an element of romance.

Only later did we begin to get clues that the version that we heard was highly edited, sanitized for the impressionable ears of children. Mom is not technically a Holocaust survivor, as her family left Eastern Europe in 1931. But her experience is in many ways similar, as her parents escaped an increasingly violent and anti-Semitic world, only to experience a life of hardship in their new home. They were separated from family, first by miles and then, in too many cases, by the brutal deaths of those they had left behind. And our mother's silence on the details is much like that of Holocaust survivors. For years she protected us. As we grew older, some details began to emerge and then, finally, she gave us the gift of these memoirs so that we—and our children and the generations to follow—would understand whence we came.

Her family's story is one of adversity of a kind unimaginable to her upper middle class progeny. From a relatively affluent life in Poland where they had businesses, servants, and nannies; her family was thrust into subsistence farming in the wilds of Argentina, living without benefit of electricity or running water. And the years ahead were strewn with one obstacle after another.

Yet this is not a story of woe. What emerges are grit, determination, imagination, gratitude and love. With no school that went beyond third grade in their county, yet determined that their children should get an education, our grandparents sent our mother and then her sister Sonia away to school when they were 10. Mom relates here that she boarded with families (each year a different one in a different town) who provided meals but no parenting. She was left on her own to occupy herself and solve problems. And solve problems she did—cooking a chicken without benefit of either experience or cookbook after the woman with whom she was boarding had a baby; finding her way home when she had diphtheria (a desperate solution highly inconsistent with public health principles); and passing tests to get to the next level in school, defying predictions that she could not succeed.

There are many heroes in this story. Despite the privation of their daily existence, our grandparents maintained the vision that their daughters were destined for a better life. The extended family rallied to help each other whenever needed. All shaken from their roots and also living in dire circumstances, many of our mother's teachers taught their students with dedication.

The story contains one villain, Baron Maurice de Hirsch, the wealthy Jew who founded the Jewish Colonization Association, which rescued Jews from Europe and settled them in rural Argentina. He was given to idiosyncratic theories about the need for Jews to be humble farmers, which included living under primitive conditions and forgoing education. Though he died long before our family arrived in Argentina, his ideas prevailed in his organization. He had felt that families should be separated, and they were deliberately located far apart.

The result was cruel. Our grandmother's sister and her family were half an hour away on horseback, and our grandfather's brother's farm was at the farthest ends of the colony from my grandparents, depriving them all of the help and comfort they might have shared. Mother has devoted a whole chapter to Baron de Hirsch, because she feels that others need to understand the damage wrought so unnecessarily by this minor figure in Jewish history, even as he was saving the lives of Jews desperate to leave Europe.

But most of the people who inhabit this story are family and friends with whom Mom shared close ties. Those relationships unfolded for us over the years. In 1962, we went to Israel for the first time, and Jessica went several times in the next several years. We were welcomed as close family into the home of Mom's cousin Nechama, her husband Yaakov, and their 4 children. When Jessica went back as a college student, their home became her second home; their daughter Tsipi, her friend. On one trip to Israel, Jessica arrived exhausted after a journey lasting almost a day and went straight to bed—only to find that she had travelled half way around to world to sleep in a bed outfitted with familiar color-splashed Marimekko sheets, courtesy of one of Mom's care packages.

Mom's memoir illuminates her close relationship with Nechama, so close that they would share a single bed on visits even as teenagers. Jessica once interviewed Nechama and asked who her best friend was growing up. She paused only a second before a smile lit up her face. "Your mother," she said.

Various Argentinian and Israeli relatives visited us over the years, and Mom fed them, sheltered them and, if they were moving here, helped them settle in.

In her teens, Wendy spent a summer in Argentina with Mom's cousin Aron Penchansky and his family. She went to school with her cousin Pompi every day. Her trip included an excursion to the "campo", the countryside, to visit Mom's cousins Benito and Jacobo Guirchovich and his family on the farm on which they had been raised, where they still had no electricity or indoor plumbing. As her hosts spoke no English, Wendy became so fluent in Spanish that Mom remembers that, on her return, she came off the plane speaking Spanish to her. Jessica travelled back and forth to Israel, and later Ken went to Argentina with Mom and his daughter Lily. On every trip, family welcomed us with love. And then the next generation began to travel on their own. When Jessica's daughter Talia spent a semester in Buenos Aires, she quickly found a home away from home with her grandmother's cousin Rosita.

In 2005 we took a family trip to Argentina to celebrate Mom's 80th birthday. In Buenos Aires, we visited cousins from both sides of her family. In Parana, in the province of Entre Rios where Mom was raised, 50 family members, many of whom we had never heard of, feted us with their homemade specialties in a penthouse office. And everywhere we went our cousins patiently accommodated the vegetarians among us—even though we eschewed their prized Argentinian beef.

We visited her cousins on the "campo,"which now had running water and electricity. Her cousin Jacobo was dressed in bombacha trousers and alpargata shoes and sported large knives handily tucked in the back of his pants, all marks of a gaucho. After they served us a feast, we asked if we could see the house our mother's family had lived in. We hopped into trucks, because cars could not make the trip on the dirt roads. The route included a bridge that was broken. Because there had been no rain, we were able to pass on the dry beds. We asked Mom how they used to get by when it rained. "That," she said, "was a problem." In the past when Mom had referred to growing up in the wilderness, we thought it was an exaggeration. Now we began to understand when she meant.

And we gradually began to understand other things. We had long considered ourselves lucky to have extended family in so many parts of the world, cousins distant in relationship, geography and experiences who nonetheless welcomed us warmly, as if we were members of their world. And we took that welcome for granted. Reading the memoir and meeting so many people who told us how deeply they loved Enia (Mom's childhood name) made clear that the depth of relationship was no accident.

Our mother was good to members of her family growing up. Maybe making up for the childhood she was denied due to circumstance, she nurtured everyone—not only her younger sisters, her cousins and eventually her children, but also her parents. And remembering her gratitude to her aunt Leike, whose care packages to her family in Argentina sustained them, she dispersed her own care packages throughout the world.

She became the glue that bound the family together. Having orchestrated a trip to Argentina for her husband, children and grandchildren, she then coaxed her sisters into trips with her. Neither had returned before. Now Sonia has taken her own family. Her granddaughter Kira spent a semester in Buenos Aires and, taking her cue from Talia, spent many happy hours with Rosita and her family. Now Lily is spending several months in Argentina, and she, too, is enjoying the warm welcome of her cousins.

Who would have thought that in just one generation, our family could move from toil and abject poverty to comfortable upper middle class life in the US? We have the vision of our grandparents and the pluck of our mother to thank.

And for the on-going relationships with family, we credit our mother. We understand now that the love we are received with is no accident, but the legacy of her investment. Nechama, Rosita, Pompi, Tsipi and their families have all become major figures in our own lives, expanding our universe, enriching our lives, welcoming us with transcendent love, whose source we now understand.

Thank you, Mom, for your love and this memoir. Publishing it is our gift to you.

Jessica, Kenneth, and Wendy

A note on names:

Ann's family name is spelled three different ways in the memoir as they changed continents and languages: as Girszowicz in Poland, as Guirchovich when referred to his brother's family in Argentina, and as Girson, the name they used in the United States.

Her cousins' name is spelled "Pieczanski" in Europe. Some members of the family retained that spelling in Argentina but others changed the spelling to "Penchansky."

1 ROOTS: THE OLD COUNTRY

As far back as I can trace my ancestors, they lived in the same geographical area, the Baranovich oblast (district), Minsk gubernya (province). However, this area did not always belong to the same country. After every war another country ruled it. Just in the 20th century, it was part of Russia, Poland and Belarus. That is not including the changes that occurred during the wars when it was overrun and ruled by additional countries.

Snov, where my mother's family lived, is situated at the intersection of two major trade routes, half way between the cities of Baranovich and Niesviz. Baranovich is twelve miles to the west of Snov and Niesviz is 13 miles east of Snov. The history of Snov is a tale of being bought and sold as part of a series of noblemen's estates. Names such as Radzivill, Rdultovsky and Gustav Gartnik come up in the literature I have been able to find. Several palaces were built and destroyed in Snov. There were recurrent political upheavals, besides major wars. Snov found itself often on the frontier and damaged or destroyed by one or the other side. It still had a surviving palace at the time I lived there. I don't think there was a nobleman living in it. I remember going there with Manya, my nanny, to play in the gardens.

We had relatives living in Baranovich and in Niesviz. I know I was taken to Niesviz, but I don't have any clear recollections. I have vivid memories of visits to Baranovich. My aunt Michla and cousin Misha lived there. I looked forward to those visits. It was an exotic place where I was entertained and treated to city experiences. We stayed at the Ghiens' home. They were my mother's relatives, probably distant ones. They had a house near where Aunt Michla and Misha lived. I remember Mr. Ghien with a strange contraption on his head sitting in front of a box. That was my first encounter with a radio. I also

1

remember Nissan, the Ghiens' son. I do not have an image of Mrs. Ghien. Mostly, I recall being happy in their home. Nissan Ghien was the only member of his family to survive the Holocaust. After the war he made his way to Italy, with the help of a Jewish organization. Misha heard from him but lost track of him.

Misha, who was six years older than I, was my idol. He was clever and funny, and full of mischief. He let me follow him around. He often came to Snov and entertained the children. He put on shows for which he charged admission. I loved being his sidekick. Among the stories of Misha's inventive pranks, not from memory, but often heard repeated, is a story about a goat. Misha gathered a paying crowd to watch him get a goat to eat paper. With the help of Uncle Honye's green sunglasses, which he put on the goat, he succeeded in getting the goat to eat shredded paper. In his later years while reminiscing, Misha told me that the visits to Snov supplied him with pocket money. When his pocket money ran out, it was time for a visit to Snov where he was sure to replenish it.

My maternal grandfather, Alter Mishkin, was born in 1865 in Snov. Zeide Alter had been an orphan for a number of years when, at nineteen, he married Bobbe Sarah in 1884. Bobbe Sarah's maiden name and birthplace I have not been able to find. My eldest cousin, Yenie, now in her nineties, lived near our grandparents until she was fifteen. She remembers them well. She knows Bobbe Sarah was not from Snov, probably from Minsk, she thinks.

Alter had an older sister, Perle, who had taken charge of him after the deaths of their parents. She expected to be consulted about his choice of a bride. Alter disappointed her. He brought a bride from elsewhere, fait accompli. Perle disapproved of Sarah and interfered in the couple's married life. At one point, she succeeded to separate them and take charge of their baby, Feigl. The story goes that Alter eventually realized that Perle was not a good mother even to her own children and equally neglectful of his Feigl. He went to Minsk, where Sarah was living, brought her back and reestablished a home. Now Sarah proved to be equal to the task of dealing with her sister-in-law. Alter and Sarah had a long marriage. They had ten children of whom seven lived to adulthood. They were Feigl, Anna, Manya (Michla), Willie, Leike, Sam and Dora.

Alter and Sara Mishkin

Sometime during the 1880's, Alter traveled to the United States to consider the possibility of immigration. He came back within a few months having decided that it was not for him. He stayed in Snov and, on a modest level, the family prospered. The important thing to him was not to work for someone else. He instilled that principle into his two sons, Willie and Sam. Sam undoubtedly would have fared better had he not followed his father's advice. Alter was enterprising and resourceful. He dealt with the local landed gentry, supplying the goods they needed to run their estates.

Time proved him wrong, however. One by one his children emigrated to the New World, some when they were still in their mid-teens. There was no future for them in Snov. Five went to the United States. Michla did not like America and returned. In 1918 she married Solomon Zamanski. He was not from the Snov area. They settled in Snov and had a son, Misha, born in 1919. Solomon was a communist and active in the Bolshevik revolution. Once the Poles took over the area, it was not safe for him to stay in Snov. He took Michla and Misha to Odessa in Russian-ruled Ukraine. Within a couple of years, the marriage was not going well. Solomon was absorbed in revolutionary politics and neglectful of his wife and child. When word came about the situation, Alter and Sarah decided to bring Michla and Misha back to Snov.

Dora, who was then in her early twenties, was dispatched to accomplish the mission. It entailed crossing the border illegally, twice. Dora arrived at the Zamanskis' and soon fell ill with typhoid fever. It took several months for her to recover enough to undertake the trip back. I heard my mother tell this story many times--the stealing across the border in the dark of the night led by a hired guide, wondering whether he was going to rob them and leave them stranded.

Solomon Zamanski continued his work for the revolution. He never saw his son again. According to Misha, his father was executed by the Communists for betraying the Party. When my family left for Argentina in 1931, the only descendants of Alter and Sarah Mishkin left in Europe were Michla and Misha. They were living in Baranovich. Misha finished the gymnasium (lyceum) there. Twenty-eight days before Hitler's armies attacked Poland, on August 3, 1939, Misha left for the United States. Aunt Leike managed to get him out in time. Unfortunately, she was not able to get a visa for Michla in time to save her.

Michla perished in the Holocaust. Misha in his note to me writes "According to my friends who survived, the Germans forcibly assembled all the Jews in the center of Baranovich and

4

machine gunned them down. My mother was among them. They were all buried in a mass grave under a bridge named *Zielony Most*." A detail Misha added was that the Germans enlisted the local Poles and commandeered them to do the killing.

In 1922 Alter and Sarah went to the United States with the intention of settling there. They made arrangements to take their two youngest children, Sam and Dora. Sam wanted to take his girlfriend, Sonia, with him and talked Dora into postponing her trip, so he could use her ticket. Before arrangements were made to replace her ticket, Dora met Benjamin Girszowicz at the wedding of her cousin who was marrying his cousin. She fell madly in love with him. The assumption was that he fell likewise in love with her. But my sister Ines told me that in his old age he confessed to her that "strictly speaking, that was not the case. "He was in love with someone else. Both he and the young woman were too poor to marry. And here was Dora, attractive, educated and not poor.

Going to the United States was now on the back burner for Dora. Anticipating pressure not to be hasty and go join her parents, Dora and Benjamin eloped, or sort of. The ceremony did not take place in Snov. No one from the bride's family was present, although she had two sisters still living in Snov at the time. I think some of his family members may have attended. Many years later, my mother was still embarrassed when the subject came up. The way my aunts and uncles referred to this event was that Dora lost her head over a handsome fellow. Sam lived with a guilty conscience for the role he played in his sister's ending up in the Argentine wilderness. He is the one who eventually orchestrated our making it to the United States, twenty-some years later.

Once married and wanting to go together, Dora and Benjamin needed new papers. It soon became clear that it was going to take years. It was 1924 and the United States had a new immigration policy that created quotas and waiting lists. Instead of getting a visa, Dora and Benjamin got on the waiting

5

list. Dora's parents came back from the United States to sort out the situation.

Zeide Alter undertook to equip the couple with the means to make a living while waiting for the visa. For Benjamin, he was able to find a non-Jew willing to lease his state license to run a liquor store. The Polish government did not give a license to a Jew, but a Jew was allowed to lease one from a non-Jew. For Dora, Zeide Alter worked out a partnership to run an officers' club. Being near the border, Snov had a military station, hence the need for an officers' club. The partners were a Jewish couple. How that license was worked out I do not know. I am sure there was some similar deal. Both enterprises turned out to be profitable. Economically they were prospering.

I was born in March of 1925. My mother went back to work and hired a nanny, Genya, to care for me. I was two when Genya left. My second nanny was Manya, who also took care of my sister Sonia, born in January 1929.

Sonia, Dora, Enia and Benjamin

Manya stayed with us until we left for Argentina in 1931. I have images of Manya taking me to see my parents at work and to play with my friend Lisa. Lisa was the daughter of my mother's partners. She was my age. Another memory is of

Manya and me going to deliver Sabbath gifts of hallah and pastry on Friday afternoon to poor families.

Enia and Lisa

My mother talked about those years with profound longing. Those were the last good years of her life. She never again had any comfort or security. In her papers after she died, I found a poem she had written in the early years in Argentina. Reading it broke my heart.

My father, on the other hand, talked about that period as sitting comfortably on a volcano knowing that it will erupt. Life was good if you did not think of the danger. He explained to me how tenuous the situation there was for Jews. The way things worked for them could not last.

Although locally the relationship between Gentiles and Jews was calm, anti-Semitism was rampant in Poland. Snov had been Russian until recently. Russian was still the language of many of its people. Both my nannies spoke only Russian. I never learned to speak Polish. Russian is what we spoke at home. The Jews were not the only minority, because the Russians were not at home there. That must have helped. In Snov there was an accommodation or understanding between the Jews and the local power structure. They had worked out a way to minimize the effects of the harsh anti-Semitic directives that came from the government. For instance, the chief of police was questioned if a period of time passed and a Jewish businessman had not been arrested and fined. The chief would call the business people together to choose whose turn it was to spend a night in jail and pay a fine. Sometimes he did it as a preventive measure, in order not to be questioned. Poland was very poor. The government needed a scapegoat and the Jews were the easiest target.

In late 1925 Alter and Sarah made their last trip to the United States. They spent the rest of their lives living in the Bronx. Four of their children were living in New York, Anna, Leike, Willie and Sam. The eldest and the youngest of their children (Feigl and Dora) ended up in the Argentine wilderness. Zeide Alter died in 1944. Bobbe Sarah died in 1946, just a couple of months before we arrived in the United States.

My paternal ancestors came from the same region, just a few miles away from Snov. My father grew up with his grandparents around him. He still remembered them clearly at the age of ninety, when I asked him to tell me about them. My father's mother, Libe, was the daughter of Abraham and Rishel Haskelevich. She had three brothers and three sisters. The family lived on the land of the estate of Count Rezevski, near Tsirin. Their income came from producing and selling cheese. They made a type of Swiss cheese. They bought the milk for the cheese from the estate, which had a herd of cattle.

8

Benjamin's parents Ephraim and Libe,
his sister Yente behind

My father's father, Ephraim, was the son of Zavel and Sheyne
Girszowicz. They lived in Tsirin. My father remembered Bobbe
Sheine as very thin, very bossy and a big doer. Zavel and
Sheyne had an inn in Tsirin and a variety of other little
businesses. With hard work and ingenuity they were able to
provide for their family. They raised seven children, four sons
and three daughters.

Zavel died before reaching the age of sixty. Ephraim, the eldest
son took over the running of the inn and the other businesses,
with Bobbe Sheyne's help and interference. Bobbe Sheyne lived
with Ephraim and Libe for many years, to the age of 85. She
saw to it that each of her children was "well established." She

apparently was not easy on her husband and was accused of sending him to his early grave. Her response to the accusation was "don't worry, when I join him the score will be evened." In old age she became forgetful and unaware that she was no longer in charge. She often distributed things that did not belong to her. Her daughter-in-law, Bobbe Libe, must have had quite a time with her. When my father related to me these recollections about his Bobbe Sheyne, I was puzzled by his evident affection for her. She was his Bobbe.

My father, Benjamin Girszowicz, was the second child born to Ephraim and Libe Girszowicz. The exact year of his birth remains a mystery. It is somewhere between 1892 and 1898. He changed his date of birth so many times that in the end he lost track of which one was the true one. In 1917, to avoid serving in the army, he made himself younger. Then came the Bolsheviks and his age was just what they were calling up, so he made himself much older. He went on to change his age several more times. When I was growing up I recall that my father's date of birth was September 14, 1898. Later I was told the year was 1897. In his documents the year is 1892.

Benjamin's eldest sibling was Yente, who was nearly ten years old when he was born. His birth was cause of great jubilation, another child at last, and a boy! But in time more children arrived: Sarah, Hanne and Abraham. Abraham had a stillborn twin sister. Twins ran in the family. There were many twins among my father's cousins.

During World War I, Russian soldiers came into Tsirin and ordered everyone to evacuate their homes and leave. The people left for the woods. When they were about a kilometer from town, they saw the whole town go up in flames. Tsirin was burned to the ground. Besides the seven family members, Bobbe Libe brought along a paralyzed old woman who had nobody to care for her. They survived in the woods for a couple of months, until fall, when they went to the town of Mir. They rented a house and lived in Mir from 1915 to 1918. In 1918 they went back to Tsirin, leased land in nearby Negivich and farmed until, not long after, the Bolsheviks put them out. They went to Haradischk for a short while and then, at last, moved back to Tsirin, which was now in Poland. The war was over. Back in Tsirin, Ephraim and Libe reestablished themselves and eventually rebuilt their house.

During this period my father was arrested by the Bolsheviks. He was accused of undermining the revolution. It had to do with some trading he was doing. He was held in the Bolshevik headquarters, questioned, and threatened with execution. After a few days they released him without explanation. The World War I experience was at the core of my father's fear of staying there and the desperate wish to get out, hence the decision to take his family to Argentina instead of waiting for a visa to the United States.

In the same region, a few miles away, lived my mother with her family. The only references to the World War I were dangerous border crossings, disruptions when ruling power changed and scarcities of some goods. My mother was away at school all through the war. I am puzzled. I wish I could find the explanation for the difference.

Once at home, the Girszowicz family's life proceeded in a normal way. Yente married Abraham Tratsovitsky. They had five children. Their youngest child was deaf. Hanne married Leibe Singarovsky. They had two daughters. Sarah never married. She lived at home with her parents and cared for them in their old age. They had built a large house, part of it for rental, to insure income in later years. Poland was not a great place for Jews. It was home nevertheless. The worst was yet to come.

I do not remember my Zeide Ephraim and Bobbe Libe or anyone else in my father's family who was left in Europe. I saw them infrequently and I lost all memories of them. All I have are their images on the few photographs we have. We don't have any of the letters that they sent us in Argentina.

Except for the sons, Benjamin and Abraham, who left for Argentina in 1931, and Hanne's husband who made it to the

United States hoping to bring his wife and daughters, the members of the Ephraim and Libe Girszowicz family were living in or near Tsirin when the Nazis arrived. There were many other relatives living in the area. The Nazis rounded up all the Jews in the Tsirin area and herded them off to Novogrudok where they were gunned down and buried.

Forty-two of my father's relatives died that day. Only two miraculously survived. I remember the day my father learned the details. I can recall only part of the date of the slaughter, February 2. I am confused about the year. I am still trying to find it. The survivors were Sholom Gulkow, my father's first cousin and Israel Tratsevitsky, a nephew, son of father's sister Yente. Sholom was buried to the neck in the mass grave. He managed to survive two days until freeing himself. Not able to walk he crawled into hiding in the woods. He witnessed the beatings, shootings and other atrocities inflicted by the Nazis on the helpless Jews. His young wife and baby were among the dead.

After the war Sholom was brought to the United States by his brother Eddie Weiss and his two sisters. In time he remarried and lived a quiet normal life in New York. Sholom talked readily about his experiences. He had a cheerful disposition. As the winters became too hard on his war damaged health, he and his wife began to spend time in Florida. While riding his bicycle in the Florida sunshine, he was hit by a car and killed. He was in his sixties.

Israel Tratsevitsky went to Israel where he met and married Boomie Gulkow, a cousin, daughter of his great aunt Peshke. They settled there and had a son.

At the end of 1925, after my grandparents left for the United States, the only other Mishkin left in Snov was my mother's eldest sibling, my aunt Feigl. Feigl was married to Honye Pieczanski and they had six children by then. Their youngest was born in 1927, months before they left for Argentina. They are the relatives that I grew up with in Argentina. Why they did not go to the United States, was never explained to me. All

Feigl's siblings went or had planned to go. And Uncle Honye's brother went. But, when the agents of the Jewish Colonization Association came to recruit families to become farmers in Argentina, they were ready to go.

2. ARGENTINA: THE EARLY YEARS

On May 3, 1931, my parents Benjamin and Dora Girszowicz, my two-year-old sister Sonia, I aged six, and my father's brother Abraham, set out from our home in Snov, Poland, for the long journey to Argentina. I remember the crowd gathered to see us off, following the horse-drawn carriage on our way to the train station. I know we stopped off in Warsaw. We have a photograph taken in Warsaw of a large group of people going on the same voyage.

Dora, Sonia and, Enia; Benjamin in Europe

From Warsaw, again by train, we went to the port of Amsterdam to board the liner SS Gelria for the ocean crossing to Buenos Aires. I have some memory of the sea voyage, playing with the other children, eating unfamiliar foods, a world of new wonders, but marred by seasickness – my mother especially, lying in her bunk in visible pain. The sea voyage took about two weeks.

We arrived in Buenos Aires in the latter part of May. Sonia had broken out in some kind of rash and was not allowed to disembark. After some negotiations, the plan was for my mother to accompany Sonia to a special hospital for communicable diseases and the rest of us to go our way. In Buenos Aires, we had some distant relatives or relatives of relatives. We stayed with them a few days, waiting for my mother and Sonia. How my father found Sonia and my mother without anyone's help in a strange big city, not knowing a word of the language, is in the annals of our family's horror stories. He found them, Sonia's rash had disappeared, and we were off on the last leg of our voyage to the place where we were to settle.

Sonia and Enia

I do not remember any part of the trip from Buenos Aires to the Province of Entre Rios. I do know that it was a long tiresome journey in those days. Several train changes, crossing the Parana River on a boat, and waiting time at every change.

We arrived at the train station of Alcaraz where my cousin met us. My mother's eldest sibling, Feigl, her husband, Honye, and their seven children had arrived in Argentina three and a half years earlier. Feigl was 15 years older than my mother. My aunt Feigl's older children (Yenie, David, Jacobo and Rive, also known as Rebeca) were closer (or as close) in age to my mother than to me. But the three younger ones, Mote (Marcos), Nechama and Aron were near my and Sonia's ages.

I do remember the events of that day. Riding in the horse-drawn wagon in a vast emptiness sticks in my mind. It was a strange place. I recall a feeling of being taken farther and farther away from my world. I remember one of my cousins pointing and saying "this is our place," and I thinking that it cannot be because there was no town. All I could see was a ramshackle building standing alone in the void. We arrived and the whole family surrounded us. The most vivid detail still with me is of a shy little girl standing at a distance looking at me. She was Nechama, my cousin. This was the beginning of our lifelong close friendship.

I had left my close friend Lisa in Snov. Nechama took her place. Lisa was the daughter of my parents' partners and the same age as I. We were constant companions from infancy. I knew that my father tried very hard to talk her parents into leaving with us. He was so convinced that staying was terribly risky. But it didn't work. Had my parents written to them that our living conditions were acceptable, they probably would have followed us. I believe my father would have done so, even if it was far from the harsh reality, but my mother wrote the truth. They didn't come and they all perished in the Holocaust.

My aunt Feigl and her family, the Penchanskys, had arrived in Argentina late in 1927. Agents of the Jewish Colonization Association, JCA (we used ICA from the French and pronounced it "eekah") had recruited them, while they were still in Europe. They were to settle in one of the many farm colonies the ICA established in Argentina.

The ICA was founded and financed by Baron Maurice de Hirsch, a German-Jewish banker and railroad builder turned philanthropist with a mission. His mission was to eradicate

Jewish persecution by making Jews into "normal citizens." He believed that the Jewish dislocation was due to the fact that Jews had gotten away from working the land, as normal people do. To that end he devised and implemented an ambitious plan. He bought large tracts of land in Argentina and some in Brazil and Canada. He created the Jewish Colonization Association to establish and administer the colonies.

The Penchanskys were now living and working on an ICA farm in a colony called Louis Oungre in a section of it called La Gama. Louis Oungre had been a director of the ICA. La Gama (The Doe) was an indigenous name. Every cluster of farms had an indigenous name, usually a name of a tree or an animal.

The first colonies were named for members of the Hirsch family and, when they exhausted that list, for directors of the ICA, who were German, French or English Jews. The main headquarters of the ICA was in Paris until World War II when it was moved to London.

The Penchanskys had arrived before the new colony was ready. They lived temporarily in one of the older colonies on a small parcel of land. Then when the new colony was established, they were among the first settlers in it. Their farm was situated next to where the schools were to be built. Eventually it would be at the center of the social life of the colony. The ICA took its time in providing for education or other such luxuries. In 1932 two one-room schools were ready, one a regular government school, all subjects taught in Spanish, the other providing Jewish education, taught in Yiddish. Each had an adjacent house for the teacher. Each teacher taught three grades simultaneously.

The Penchanskys lived in a corrugated iron barnlike structure. They had added a lean-to to provide us with a place to stay until we were ready to move to our own farm. The local ICA administration assigned us a site in a far corner of the colony called El Chanar. It was on high land, an arroyo (stream) running through it, but to reach it one needed to cross a small river. They promised to build a bridge soon. The entire 200 acres were densely covered with trees and, what is more significant, with a particularly pernicious, hard to uproot, type of palm.

Clearing the land for farming was among the travails my father would remember in old age with all the emotion of a recent disaster. Forty-five years later, while we were living in Manhattan, my father came from Brooklyn to visit us and his eyes fell on a large palm my husband had just given me for my birthday. He stood speechless fixedly looking at it with an incredulous expression on his face. "Do you know what this is?" he finally said, and continued: "Did you pay money for this?" When I tried to explain, he shook his head in disbelief. "This was the bane of my life in Argentina," he said with tears in his eyes.

Our stay with the Penchanskys lasted several months. I remember learning to speak Yiddish, the lingua franca of the colony. The farmers had come from many different countries and Yiddish was the common language until the young generation changed it to Spanish.

One family, the Sauls, who came from Cyprus but were Palestinian Jews, arrived without any knowledge of Yiddish. They spoke only Hebrew. They had quite a time learning two languages simultaneously. The rest had no easy time either. The Yiddish spoken was so varied, people had to familiarize themselves with the different dialects in order to understand each other. I recall my father reporting after a conversation in Yiddish with a neighbor, saying, "I doubt that we were on the same subject". At the same time they needed to learn Spanish fast because they depended on the local population to survive in that wilderness. Very few of them had any familiarity with horses, much less how to tame wild ones. How they withstood the rigors of getting started to produce the bare necessities for survival remains beyond my comprehension.

As an adult, I rationalized that the total disregard for suffering displayed by the ICA was due to mismanaged bureaucracy. However, when I researched the history of the ICA, I found that that was the policy from the beginning. They were modeling the Jewish farmer after the Eastern European peasants. Poverty and misery was normal. That is how Baron de Hirsch set forth to achieve the normalization of the Jewish people. He was not on a mercy mission. He had higher ideals.

In his autobiographical book Yitzhak Kaplan, a man who spent his whole life in the cooperative movement of the colonies trying to ameliorate the harshness of the farmers' lot, describes the treatment that his own family received in 1895 when they came to the colonies. His parents and their seven sons came under the auspices of the ICA. It took them seven weeks to travel from their hometown of Sislewicz (near Bialystok) to Buenos Aires. There were a number of changes before they boarded the cross-Atlantic liner. At each change there was a representative of the ICA, and, at the hands of each one of them, they received inconsiderate and degrading treatment. There were five families in the group. The observance of kashruth caused them great hardship. This was compounded by the insulting attitude of the agents.

When they finally landed in Buenos Aires, exhausted and hungry, they begged for a place where they could get some kosher food. They were served food they believed to be kosher, but later saw a pig's head in the kitchen.

Here is a passage from Yitzhak Kaplan's book "Jewish Colonies in Argentina" (translated from Yiddish):

> "The ICA administrator of the Colony Mauricio, Yehoshua Lapin, said to them [the parents] that each family will get 50 hectares [123 acres] of land, a house, a water pump, 8 oxen, 2 cows, 2 horses and 10 chickens. You have to pay it off in 13 years. The product of your harvest the ICA takes as payment for the debt. To the question of where does the money for food and clothing for the family come from? Lapin said, about that, the homemaker is to worry. She has to make a garden, raise chickens and from the flour sacks make clothes. -- And to marry off a child? -- A child's wedding, you buy a

quart of liquor, cut up a black bread, with herring, and you celebrate a wedding."

That was in 1895, at the beginning of the colonies. By 1931, when we arrived, nothing had changed.

During the time we were living with the Penchanskys, my father and Uncle Abraham were gone from dawn to dusk, trying to ready our farm for cultivation, and supervising the building of our house. My cousins David, age 20, and Jacobo, age 18, were in the fields doing the plowing and other preparation for seeding in September (early spring). Plowing was done with a horse-drawn single blade plow. It took forever to plow one of those big fields. Before any other work came milking the cows. In the winter, it was done while still dark, with a lantern for light. The day was extended as much as possible because it was never long enough to do all the work, more so in winter. We were at the comparable latitude of northern Florida. Winter nights were not that long, but the workload too heavy to adjust to any decrease in time.

Aunt Feigl, my mother, my cousins Yenie, age 21, and Rive, age 16, and the five younger children, ages two to nine, were around the house. The women were responsible for the care of the chickens and other small farm animals, watering the large animals kept nearby for special purposes, and a myriad of other chores. Water was pumped by hand into pails and carried. And then there was food preparation. Nothing came prepared. Bread was made, starting with the flour, mixing the ingredients, kneading, leaving it to rise, and finally baking it in a brick oven preheated with a wood fire. Everything was labor-intensive. Noodles were made by hand. But the biggest problem was having enough supplies.

That is where my mother first got a whiff of what her life as a farmer's wife would be. She learned very well. My father was to become a model farmer, in large part due to my mother who was an extraordinary farmer's wife. She was terribly unhappy, but fought like a tigress to survive with a semblance of civilization.

These drastic changes in our lives transformed my relationship to my parents. From a carefree childhood I went to the realization that my parents were not in control of what happens to us. I only understood partially what had happened, but not why. I knew that my mother was forced to leave her comfortable life and come to this place. I had enormous compassion for her. I identified with her sorrow. When I was older I was able to put together the sequence of events that brought us there.

By 1930 we had been on the United States immigration waiting list for over five years. My father was getting more and more concerned about the wait, and the answers to the inquiries were not optimistic. He was desperate to get out of Poland. He was convinced that another European war would break out before long. He reasoned that, with the virulent anti-Semitism raging in Poland, the Jews would be the ones to suffer most. He was determined to get his family out of its path. When the agents of the ICA had come previously and the Penchanskys and many relatives and friends signed up, he apparently had not given it a thought. Now when the agents returned he decided to go. When he broke the news to my mother, she told him she was not going. She wanted to wait for the visa to the USA. When he saw that he could not convince her, he told her that he was ready to take the girls and go without her. By Polish law, he had the right.

We were not ideal candidates for the ICA colonies. A middle-class business couple with two daughters did not constitute a good prospect for carrying out the ICA's mission. Uncle Abraham's coming along made us more acceptable. The ICA extracted a security deposit from my father, besides payment for the passages.

I have thought about my aunt Feigl, who must have written letters to my mother, not telling her how dismal a place it was. But knowing my aunt Feigl, it is not hard to see that it was entirely in character. She was not capable of complaining. She was one of those rare people, who despite almost everything going wrong in her life, walked this earth full of love and hope.

We lived with the Penchanskys through the winter. I have vivid pictures of some incidents that happened during those few months. Cooking was done outside on an open fire, even in cold weather. Beef was the staple diet in the region. If you could afford anything, you could afford beef. There was little besides what you could produce yourself. The Spaniards had brought cattle to Argentina in the 16th century and let them loose in the fertile lands. For a long time there was a very small population of Europeans.

The Indian population fared very badly under Spanish rule. It is only in recent years that the truth has come out, that the Spaniards nearly wiped out the Indian population in most of the country. Many Indians died from diseases introduced by the conquerors, others died from the harsh treatment they were subjected to, and untold millions were just killed. There were no Indians left in the fertile plains. The remnants of the Indian population remain to this day in the far reaches of the mountains, the jungle and the frigid territories of the south.

The cattle flourished. They were hunted like wild game. The natives told stories about people killing a cow because they wanted meat for a barbecue, leaving the rest of the carcass in the field. The ICA bought some of the land with cattle on it. This does not mean that the settlers got any cattle free of charge. With the ICA there was no such thing as free of charge. Cattle, however, were relatively cheap.

With no refrigeration, the diet was extremely limited. In winter there were potatoes, sweet potatoes, carrots, beets, onions from the garden, but rarely all them. To have a successful crop you had to plant many different ones. Just as the soil and the climate were kind to growing vegetation, they were also kind to the pests who love to eat them. As there were no pesticides, one prayed that the pests would ignore some of the vegetables. Milk was the other available product, but there were no other milk products because the needed machinery for processing was not available.

My aunt Feigl was religious and her husband came from a traditional family. He had had a comprehensive Jewish education and had a good voice. Holiday observances at the Penchanskys were very special. Not much else good could be said about Tio Honye, as I called him. He excelled at eschewing work and all family responsibilities. I don't think he loved anyone other than himself. But my aunt Feigl, who loved all God's creatures, loved him dearly. She even managed to have the children care for him and treat him with respect. The children got all their love from their mother and grew up to be the best of parents. Aunt Feigl also managed to instill in her children a deep caring for each other. It was this bond that saw them through unbelievable hardships to make their way in life.

Now, back to the winter of 1931: 14 of us are living in this wilderness in dire straits and my aunt Feigl is thinking about kashruth. There was no shohet within hundreds of miles, no refrigeration, no paved road, and there was a shortage of money. Aunt Feigl decides that by bending the rules here and there she can still follow her God's will and not harm her family. She proceeds by treating the meat as if it had been from an animal slaughtered by a shohet, using only the kosher parts and salting the meat as ritual dictates.

One memorable Saturday, in the spirit of bringing in as much tradition as possible, a cholent that had been prepared was being readied for serving. The household was agog with excitement. Yenie, the eldest of Feigl's children, was putting the final touches to the daunting undertaking. She lifted a container she thought was of oil and poured some in the pot. She smelled kerosene and realized what she had done. The scene of sadness that followed hasn't faded in my memory in the 7 decades since it took place. Everything edible was in that cholent.

The time came for us to move to our own farm. Actually, we never owned it. The ICA didn't sell the land to the farmers in those days. They did finally do so in the late forties during Peron's presidency when an anti-latifundismo law was passed. Latifundismo is the system of vast land-ownership characteristic of the former Spanish colonies in South America. The ICA was cited for its large landholdings. The argument that it was a philanthropic enterprise didn't do any good. The ICA was fined a large sum of money. The conditions of the settlement included the selling of the land to the farmers.

If the reader detects my dislike of the ICA, I assure you that it is correct, and furthermore, it is so among all the people I have ever known there. To this day, we all carry the hurt of the injury inflicted on our families by the ICA. The administration of the ICA was autocratic, degrading and heartless. Hard rules, regardless how unfair, were applied without mercy. One of the strictest rules was to keep related people from having adjacent, or even nearby, farms. They placed relatives as far from each other as possible. This caused additional hardships. It made it very difficult to visit or help each other. There was an ugly system of informers. People got special favors for informing on their neighbors.

In Paiticu (the section where my Uncle Abraham and my cousin Yenie lived), there was a standoff between the farmers and the ICA administration. The farmers discovered that the teacher of the Jewish school was informing on them. Enraged, they asked for his removal. Not succeeding, they boycotted the school and hired a substitute on their own. The poor man was paid mostly in kind because the farmers did not have enough money, but he stayed.

Many families lacked food, many had no adequate winter clothing, and medical care was almost nonexistent. By the time one got to a doctor, it was often too late. This did not concern the administrators. No wonder the farmers considered the ICA their enemy. Survival was clearly dependent on helping one another. The dependence on one's neighbors was a strong unifying factor. It was enhanced by the solidarity against the common enemy. There was no recourse. When World War II broke out and the main ICA headquarters moved from Paris to London, the local administrators had an automatic excuse for the rigidity: "You know they are in exile; we cannot get any action." All through the war, the entire bureaucracy of the ICA in Argentina continued to be occupied in keeping the status quo unharmed.

We had a brick house with large windows, as my mother had specified. It consisted of three large rooms and a big porch, which in that climate we were able to use most of the year as an additional all-purpose room. The house did not have any plumbing or wiring. Our source of water was a pump across the road, on our future neighbor's land. Consistent with its policy, the ICA insisted on putting it across the road, even though that farm was not assigned yet. Any way of wielding power over the farmer, making sure that his life was not made too easy, was modus operandi.

My mother unpacked the steamer trunks and put up lace curtains. She covered the plain beds with beautiful bedspreads, put photographs on the walls, covered the plain table with a cloth, and in general, made the house into a pretty home. My father, with the help of the veteran farmers, acquired equipment, cattle, horses, some chickens and whatever else was essential to establish the farm. My parents had brought some money from Europe. My father had also deposited money with the ICA agents in Europe. I don't know whether he ever saw any of it again. It probably went to pay for debts incurred. Farmers were always in debt to the ICA. We had a running start compared with most of the colonists who had arrived penniless. For some, the ICA paid the passage over and expected repayment. They lived in unbelievable deprivation for years with the ICA constantly on their backs demanding payments.

My mother had brought large quantities of clothing, household linens and anything else she could think would be useful in the New World. She also brought her fur coat and my father's fur-lined one. I recall an incident when my father arrived freezing from a trip to the village of Alcaraz. My mother took him to task for not wearing the fur-lined coat, as she had asked him to do. He became angry and gave her a lecture about the morality of showing up in such a coat among people who don't own a jacket. I don't remember my mother ever wearing her fur coat.

Soon after we moved to our own place, my father and the Penchansky boys went on a long overnight trip and brought back a wagon-full of paraiso saplings to plant around the houses. Paraiso is a large tropical tree with exuberant aromatic flowers. Its name, paradise, is truly descriptive of its beauty and beneficence. It is an excellent shade tree and an impressive sight. In time our house was in a forest of paraisos. The trees grew fast and before long they were touching each other's branches. I can still feel the uplifting effect of waking up to the fragrance of paraisos in bloom. Approaching our place in the spring, when the paraisos were in bloom, was quite an experience. Glorious, I thought.

Nature around was far from attractive. The land was flat and although very fertile had a scrubby appearance. The look of rural poverty was everywhere--in the houses, sheds, fences, roads, vehicles, and even the people. Beauty was a rare commodity and a dramatic experience. I recall the loveliness of soft blue fields of flax in bloom and golden fields of ripe wheat waving in the wind. My father would take me to see them. We would stand and admire the radiance before us. Some of our animals were beautiful, a handsome horse, a foal, a calf, a baby chick, but in the aggregate it all spoke of poverty. My mother did everything possible to make the house surroundings as attractive as possible. The porch was full of flowering plants and a flower garden encircled the house. Fruit trees also added to the decor. What a struggle it was for her. She never gave up.

One of the early acquisitions that my parents made was a sulky. It may have been the first in the colony. A sulky is a two-wheel carriage with springs. It seats three and is drawn by one horse. It was considered a luxury. I did not know until I researched the history of the ICA what a symbol of decadence it was to them. They considered it a sign of ambition, an omen of bad tidings, the beginning of the coming apart of the mission. The farmer needed to be kept from wanting anything other than the absolute necessities for sustaining life.

The administrators were warned to watch for such signs. It was the greatest sin until someone in one of the older part of the colonies acquired a piano. I recall my mother ironically quoting an administrator, "Girszowicz may become a farmer, but the Mrs. never." The sulky must have exacerbated the low opinion in which they regarded my mother. Later, every bigwig on an inspection tour was brought to our house to show him proudly an example of success.

The cluster of farms to which ours belonged was named El Chanar. There were about ten farms in El Chanar. Each farm was approximately 200 acres in size. The houses were to be clustered in groups of four, but few of them were. Mostly, one ended up with one close neighbor. It had to do with a number of things, such as the configuration of the land, but I think, primarily because the chickens were kept loose and the farmers couldn't afford fences. Chickens are not branded. They can end up laying eggs on your neighbor's grounds or moving there altogether. In the farmer's life there was no room for social considerations.

Because we lived so far apart, it was difficult for children to have playmates. School was where children interacted with other children. Between attending the two schools we had hardly any time left. The regular school went from very early morning to midday, six days a week. The Jewish school started right after a short lunch break and lasted for the rest of the day, but just five days a week. In the beginning, some people resisted sending their children to school on Saturday, but eventually all complied.

There was one ultra-Orthodox family that didn't participate in anything. I don't know how they resolved the Saturday school attendance, since law mandated it. Their children were not allowed to play with their neighbors' children. They wanted to be left alone and people respected their wishes. One wondered how they managed to survive with such constraints in such a godforsaken place.

There was an incident that I was recently reminded of while reminiscing with my Penchansky cousins during a visit to them. The farmer whose turn it was to collect the milk containers and take them to the creamery had arrived to deliver back the empty container to this family. He saw the husband hitting his wife with a chain. He ran towards them to rescue the victim and found himself confronting her. She was angry with him for interfering in a private marital dispute. She admonished him that no one is to meddle between a husband and his wife.

At my request my father wrote a short essay on the farming experience. He was a man of few words, but he could write beautifully. He obviously had trouble with the subject. I think it was too painful. Here are a few lines of what he wrote about this period:

> "By the time we arrived, the colony did not have any clear land. We were anxious to settle down, make a home and give up the wanderer's walking stick. We did not understand what we were facing. The land we were assigned was the hardest to deal with. It had to be cleared not only of trees but also of palms that were the farmer's nemesis. It took nearly half a year of intensive work and worry before we had our little house, a source of water (a pump), some clear land to cultivate, and a few animals. We were confronting obstacles we never knew existed. Armies of hard working ants that could undo any amount of work we put in. Lack of rain during the growing season, floods during harvest time. And if all that was not enough, the seasonal visits of locust, that left black fields in its wake, having eaten up every last leaf in the whole region."

Now life for Sonia and me was lonely. At the Penchanskys we had playmates, and there were people coming and going all the time. Here we were isolated. My father and Uncle Abraham were always in the fields. My mother was so busy all day that the only way to have her company was to follow her around while she worked, which we did a lot. Our future neighbors may have still been in Europe.

But something extraordinary happened to us. Across the road in a small cabin lived two elderly men who befriended us. Before we moved to the farm, my father and Uncle Abraham had met them. They were native to the region. I don't know how my father communicated with them. They had no language in common, but these two men managed to be very helpful to my father and Uncle Abraham.

My father took Sonia and me to their place and introduced us. Don Jose and Don Francisco were their names. They were brothers and their last name was Sosa.

Don Francisco with Ines

They gave us such a warm reception that we loved them immediately. They made us toys out of readily available natural materials such as wood, sticks, pebbles, leather and feathers. In spite of not speaking our language, they were able to teach us games, also fashioned from such materials. And there always was a special treat --store-bought *caramelos* (hard candy). Later, when we learned to speak Spanish came the best of all --story-telling. We spent much of our time with them.

Don Jose and Don Francisco were woodsmen. Before the ICA acquired the land from the provincial government, it was open land. The native population was made up mostly of *criollos,* the name for descendants of Spaniards born in Argentina. There were some traces of Indian mix, but no Indians. They lived off the land freely. There were few of them and the expanses of land vast. Don Jose and Don Francisco made their living by cutting down trees, and selling the wood. Now they were too old to do much work. They had a lot of time to entertain us, and they obviously enjoyed doing it. They were extremely clever at games. I will never know whether they learned or invented them. We got attached to these men and they to us. My parents saw it and decided to ask them to move their cabin onto our farm. Otherwise they would have ended up on our neighbor's farm. They were happy to move. But soon after moving to our farm, Don Jose died. My parents asked Don Francisco to move his cabin next to our house and join our family. He lived with us until 1946, when we left for the United States.

We did not abandon Don Francisco. He went to live with the younger generation of the Penchanskys. Don Francisco had become a legend in the entire district. The Penchansky children loved him, as did any child exposed to him. He was a mesmerizing storyteller. Any child who visited us enjoyed the treat of a story told by an inventive storyteller and natural entertainer. We never knew where the stories came from. He was literate, and that was rare among the indigenous population. But he could not have read so many stories, because there were not that many books around.

There was this mystery about Don Francisco. He was this extraordinary person whom we all loved and knew nothing about. There was a tacit understanding not to question him.

He had never heard about Jews, and here we arrived en masse and he didn't care where we came from or why we were there. He just accepted us, and loved us unconditionally. Don Francisco used the words "Christian" and "person" interchangeably. He didn't know that there were people who were not "Christian." "Christian" was the word commonly used for person by all the natives. Once, when I was about 8, on a Saturday a group of Jewish men gathered to pray in our house. Don Francisco and I were sitting on the porch when one of the men came out to say that they were short one man for a minyan, and he was looking for someone to go find one. Don Francisco without hesitation volunteered to be the tenth man. Big laughter followed. Don Francisco with all sincerity responded to the laughter with "but I am a good Christian." I remember being upset about the laughter and thinking there is something unfair about a religion that would exclude such a good man. I was sure that God would not have wanted that.

When I became a mother and read Dr. Spock, I thought of Don Francisco. I felt that Dr. Spock had put in writing Don Francisco's ideas. Don Francisco believed that children are intrinsically good and if treated thoughtfully, will never need to be reprimanded. In his presence nobody was to offend a child. It was the most wonderful thing for us kids, but you can imagine what it did to our parents. At the table, if my mother or father scolded us, Don Francisco would get up and leave.

The interesting thing is that my parents never took him on. They were never jealous of him. I never asked them what made them treat him differently from anybody else. They would have never taken it from anybody else. It was the knowledge of his total devotion to their children. I know they were most grateful for it. The only derogatory comment I remember ever hearing from my parents about Don Francisco was, "he is as stubborn as a mule." It has to be said he stood his ground well. Don

Francisco didn't argue. He took a position and stood firm. And if anyone asks Sonia or me, we would say he was always right.

My parents were devoted to him and did everything possible to care for him. When he was sick, they nursed him lovingly. One time when he had the flu, my mother insisted that he stay in the room that had heating, the kitchen. It was our family room in the winter. Mother fixed him a bed with a feather quilt and installed him in it. He was not happy with the whole idea, but too sick to stand his ground. In the evening after supper, my parents started to play cards, while keeping him company. At the first complaint from one of them about what the other had done, Don Francisco wrapped himself up in the quilt and took off for his cabin.

School was about to start. It was less than two miles to school, but hard to walk and dangerous. There were many snakes, and one called *yarara* was extremely venomous. There was no bridge yet. You had to go out of the way to where the arroyo was shallow enough to wade across, that is, when the water in it was low. On horseback was the safer way to go. Don Francisco now had a new job. He found a suitable horse, a small black and white mare, which we named Tuviana. He taught me to ride, to saddle her and in general the proper way to handle her. He also escorted me to school for quite a while. When there were other children riding to school, he only came along when conditions were especially dangerous, such as the horse having to swim across the arroyo, because of high waters.

Tuviana and I got along well. I took good care of her, and she obeyed me. I never became proficient at horseback riding, just good at riding Tuviana. The schools had a large grassy area where the students let their horses loose for the day. It was fenced in and gated. After school each of us went to get our horse, saddle him and go home. Some horses were hard to catch, but Tuviana came to me as soon as she saw me.

Once, however, not only did she not come, she was nowhere to be found. I was worried and was trying to figure out what to do, when I saw Don Francisco coming on his tall horse Bayo with

32

Tuviana in tow. Tuviana apparently had gotten out through the people's turnstile and gone home. When my parents saw her without me they were frightened about what had happened to me. Don Francisco assured them that Tuviana would not have left me if I had fallen off. He calmed them down and left to pick me up. On another occasion, Tuviana proved Don Francisco right. The saddle became loose, and it moved to the side, throwing me off to the ground. I landed under her, against her legs. She stood still all the time it took me to get up, resaddle and remount her.

After three years of attending the local school, I went to the village of Alcaraz where they had a fourth grade. It was too far a ride, so I had to board with a family there. Tuviana went on to repeat three years of school with Sonia. Sonia was a natural rider. She could ride any horse with confidence and style. Sonia invented using Tuviana as you would a homing pigeon. If she decided to stay overnight at the Penchanskys and hadn't told her parents, she wrote a note, hung it on Tuviana's neck, and sent her home. Of course, the next day Don Francisco had to come to pick her up after school.

During those difficult first years of isolation and incredible hardships of all sorts, my mother worked as hard as she could and cried even harder. My father worked as hard as he could. They protected us as much as possible from the overwhelming adversities they were trying to cope with. I knew it and I grieved for them. It didn't keep me from playing make believe and having hopes. Don Francisco made up for much of the deficit.

Two teachers also brought brightness into my life. Ella Solari de Bertozzi came to her post in this forsaken place through unusual circumstances. One had to believe it was divine intervention. Mrs. Bertozzi came from Parana, the capital of the province of Entre Rios. She was born to a distinguished family, the Solaris, and married the son of the richest man in the city, Bertozzi. They were well educated, good looking, rich, and their future looked bright. His father's enterprises assured him a prominent place in the business world.

A few years, and three children later, Mrs. Bertozzi found out that her husband had gambled away more than his share of his father's fortune and her money too. Her father-in-law offered her a deal. He would take care of her and her children, if she would leave her husband. She didn't agree to that. She loved her husband and she was determined to save him. She worked out a plan. She was going to take him away from the world of gamblers to some place hard to get to and get out of. She had a degree in education. All she needed was a teaching job in such a place. That is how our one-room school got Ella Solari de Bertozzi as a teacher.

The Bertozzis took up residence in the house provided for the teacher, next to the schoolhouse. They had three daughters, two of them in their mother's school. The eldest was already past the third grade and in school in Parana. Mr. Bertozzi was a charming man, well-liked by everyone. He was an understanding and helpful partner in his wife's incredible undertaking. She set out not only to teach the children, she vaccinated, she served milk and bread, she helped when anyone was sick and with any other crisis. Mrs. Bertozzi was a self-appointed missionary. She nurtured bodies and souls. And her husband was with her all the way.

Mrs. Bertozzi was a gifted teacher. The teaching itself was difficult enough, with three grades taught simultaneously and many of the students not speaking Spanish. Besides the immigrant children, there were the indigenous ones who lived in *ranchos* (palm huts) in the woods. They were even poorer than the immigrant children. They came to school on foot and barefoot. Also, because this was the first school in the area, children up to the age of 14, some even older, were enrolled.

Mrs. Bertozzi moved heaven and earth to bring light into the life of her charges. The school was provided with little in the way of teaching materials, but she somehow gathered materials from sources in Parana where she had connections. She managed to have books to lend to her pupils. She was keenly aware that, for most of the children, this was their only chance of getting some education. Her husband tutored the older children, including some who were not registered. He also arranged all sorts of correspondence classes for the young adults. Mrs. Bertozzi arranged for some of the bright indigenous children to go to Parana to live with families, help with housework or childcare, and go to school. There were no limits to what Mrs. Bertozzi would or could do.

After I finished the third grade, I saw the Bertozzis when I was home for summer vacations. She eventually accepted a teaching position near Parana from which she later retired. The Bertozzis then moved back to Parana. The exile ended. Mr. Bertozzi died just a few years after that. So far as we knew, during all those years they lived a harmonious and loving life together. He never gambled again.

In December of 1966, I visited Mrs. Bertozzi. I had not seen her in more than twenty years. I had been apprehensive about the encounter, I feared I had idealized her image and would find her different. I needn't have worried. She was just as I remembered. Aging had not been unkind to her. She was still handsome with piercing shiny dark eyes and full of spirit. She talked about herself, her children, and grandchildren with joy and satisfaction. She wanted to know everything about me and my family. I felt as if my visit had been expected. Mrs. Bertozzi was used to having her former students come visit her. My appearance was no surprise. She knew, sooner or later, they all showed up. We picked up where we had left off and had a warm and interesting visit.

The Jewish teacher, Uri Rubinson, and his family took up residence in the house next to the Jewish school. He too was an extraordinary teacher. At that time in Argentina there were no other jobs for Jewish intellectual immigrants. That was our luck. The Rubinsons had three children, Leiser, Hillel and Rivkah. The boys were past the third grade, and were away at school except in summer. Rivkah was still a baby. The Rubinsons contributed greatly to the cultural life of the colony. They were book people. They and the Bertozzis brought light into that cultural wasteland.

Uri Rubinson was a frail man, but full of passion. He invested enormous energy into teaching his students, not just the rudiments of Yiddish, but a love for Jewish history and literature. He was not a religious man, I thought, because he did not teach us prayers. If someone wanted to learn prayers to prepare for bar mitzvah, he would gladly oblige –after school-hours and free of charge. He was able to reach his students in a way I have never again experienced. In the beginning, when most of us could not read yet, he included daily readings. The class, within a minute or two, sat as if in a trance. He chose stories or passages from literature, not necessarily children's literature, and read them with meaning and passion. I remember sitting in class with tears running down my face. Often, when the reading was finished, we were all wiping our eyes.

These readings were the greatest incentive for learning to read. Owning a book was another goal. The way both our teachers related to books made all the difference between accepting a semi-literate existence and striving to enrich our lives through books. Even after we had learned to read, our teacher continued to read to us often. He was desperate for us to learn about the world of books and we had no access to books.

Just buying textbooks was hard for our parents. Even my parents were strapped. The money they had brought was all gone now, "invested" in the farm. These were the thirties. The world economic crisis was raging. Farmers suffered because agricultural products dropped in value due to the drop in exports. No one there was established enough to withstand the rigors of the crisis. It took several years to start a book fund to purchase some books. We called it our library. I think the first acquisition consisted of thirty books. It had taken a number of sessions to agree on the list of books to purchase and the strict rules for borrowing.

The teacher sent away for textbooks and the children were to bring the money for payment. I recall an occasion when my parents didn't have the money to give me. When my name was called, I said that I did not have the money, but would bring it tomorrow. A girl named Elena Gilman, twice my size, stood up and in a loud voice said, "Those people eat meat and potatoes every day and they don't have a peso to pay for a book." I remember the scene, and how humiliated I felt. When I told my parents about the incident, they gave me an explanation that made me feel sorry for Elena.

That first group of students encompassed a wide age range, from six to fourteen or fifteen. The work that went into organizing the day to make it productive for each student must have been daunting. We loved and respected our teachers, but it was much later, upon reflection, that we realized what an incredible job our first two teachers had done. I think that we made it clear to them how much we came to appreciate it. Uri Rubinson died early in the forties when World War II was at its darkest. He had been so despondent over it that we all thought it was a contributing factor to his early death.

I have kept in touch with the Rubinson family over the years. Rivkah married Tully Friedgut, a Canadian. They have lived in various places, including Washington D.C. where I was living at the time. She and her family have lived in Israel for many years now. Rivkah was a professional multilingual translator. She has translated this memoir into Spanish.

Leiser and Hillel and their families have lived in Buenos Aires all these years. I was recently in Buenos Aires and had a chance to reminisce with Hillel about our years in the colony. To my astonishment I heard him talk about the long walk to a minyan he took with his father every Saturday. So Uri Rubinson was, after all, a religious man. I find it difficult to comprehend his abstaining from religious instruction to his pupils. It was a mystery to me until I heard of Hillel's explanation. To Uri Rubinson, going to religious services was an act of solidarity with fellow Jews. He did it out of respect and desire to encourage the participants. He valued the practice of Jewish traditions in any form.

3. FARM ECONOMICS

On our two hundred acres we grew wheat and flax for cash crop, and corn and alfalfa for the animals. We had about sixty dairy cattle, twenty some horses and five hundred chickens. There was always something growing experimentally, usually at the suggestion of an ICA agronomist. I don't recall a hit, though. We also had, for our own consumption, fruit trees, a vegetable garden and the luxury of a flower garden.

Benjamin, Dora, Enia and Sonia at the farm

One would think that it would be possible to make a decent living with such an inventory and a lot of hard work. That was not the case. The daily expenses came from selling chicken eggs. Chickens lay year round. There was a limit to how many

Dora and Sonia on a threshing machine

The maven partner went to inspect the machine and, he was, if satisfied, to make the deal. Then the three of them organized an expedition to bring the harvester home. Those harvesters were not self-driven. On the farm, horses drove them. But on the road, you needed to use a tractor. I don't remember how they got a tractor. What I remember clearly is that my father arrived home from this trip that took the better part of a week so despondent that the scene is still painful to me today. He was overcome with exhaustion, totally drained and almost speechless. He later told us about the tractor breaking down several times, being stranded on the road and people in comfortable cars whizzing by.

I do not remember any arguments among the partners, but I have recollections of breakdowns and searches for affordable replacement parts. Harvests remained problematic to the end. For small farms, harvesters were not economically viable. It is only the very large farm enterprises with the ability to mechanize that could do it successfully. But the ICA insisted on the model with which they started, regardless of the consequences. The only thing it served was the ICA's preposterous philosophy of making Jews into humble farmers without ambitions.

Locusts are a unique experience. They come in such numbers that they obscure the sun. I remember gathering all locust-edible material, rushing into the house and closing all windows and doors. After swarming, the locusts would land and start eating. Next morning we would wake up to an eerie landscape. The ground was evenly black, not a leaf left on a tree or plant, not a blade of grass. The locusts were now buried in the ground laying their eggs.

The horror of it all was awesome. The immediate task was to find the nearest place where there was food for the animals. The only ones that enjoyed the visit were the chickens. They immediately went on a high protein diet and produced eggs with flaming red yolks. I recall that there was a problem with selling those eggs. Just about the time that some growth appeared, hopping young locusts materialized, and everything got eaten up once more. When they finally left, the devastation was complete.

Locusts eat everything that grows. They also eat cloth. If one gets into your pocket, he will eat himself out before you discover his presence. Once, I had packed a valise for my trip to Buenos Aires when the locusts arrived. When I opened the valise to unpack, a locust jumped out. My two best dresses packed on top were full of holes.

After the locusts left, sadness descended on the colony. It took a lot of courage to continue. The setback was overwhelming. Then there were the stories about the unusual things that the locusts ate. They weren't funny until much later.

One year the government instituted a program to combat the locust plague. The plan was to dig up all locust eggs and destroy them. The government was to pay by the kilo for bags of locust eggs. The pay was little, but it had the effect of a gold rush. People spent long hours digging, collecting and sifting the eggs from the trenches. It had to be well sifted to assure pure locust eggs. My cousin Riveh Penchansky and her then boyfriend Shabitay Saul were the recognized champions.

There was great excitement when, having enough bags to justify a trip to the station, you went and compared your achievement to those of the other locust egg miners. It was manna from heaven. And, as often happens in gold rushes, someone was caught cheating by the inspector. The delivery was not pure enough. The details escape me, but I remember the talk about the shameful act. This experiment was never repeated. The government never again attempted to deal with the locusts.

The locusts came from Brazil. The province of Entre Rios is near its border and fertile. We had the unwanted visitors many times, not in any order that we could detect. Folklore says that locusts come for seven consecutive years, and then stay away for seven years. I have always suspected that someone used the Bible story about Joseph in Egypt to create a new folktale. Sometime after we left the colony, the locusts stopped coming altogether.

We also lived through floods and droughts. The damage inflicted by either can be devastating. I recall an occasion in the early years when we had a scary flood. We ended up with chicks in our house. Everyone was busily securing the safety of calves and other small animals.

In the midst of the goings on our farm helper showed up triumphantly dragging a *carpincho (a* type of wild hog). The inundation had washed it down our creek, and he had caught it. Don Francisco gave his stamp of approval as to the quality of a *carpincho's* meat assuring my father that it was delicious. My mother would have no part in the event. She just wanted the feast kept at a distance from the house and no utensils from the house would be used. Don Francisco and the farm help proceeded to improvise a barbecue pit on which to grill the meat.

Word went out to the neighbors to partake of the feast. I do not recall whether I ate the meat. Usually I tended to be with my mother on such occasions. She wanted and, in large measure succeeded, to cling to the traditions and customs of her former life. Sonia, who was then three or four years old, loved such occasions and joined in without questions. I, being four years older, was keenly aware of my mother's discomfort and stayed beside her.

Mother was thirty-one years old when we arrived in Argentina. Unhappy as she was, she insisted on unbelievable standards of cleanliness and grooming. It was of the utmost importance that Sonia and I grow up wearing pretty clothes. Our dresses were starched and properly ironed. She had no other help than a laundress who came once a week to do the wash by hand. She made sure that the household linen and her daughters' dresses were starched and properly ironed.

Mother soon found that she could not get all her work done from dawn to dusk. She undertook to learn to sleep fewer hours and do the housework at night. We would wake up to find fresh bread, noodles, cake, cookies or other special foods. She seldom took a siesta, which everyone else did. There was always something she felt compelled to do.

Both my parents tried to impart culture and knowledge of what the world outside had to offer. But we also absorbed much from the world around us. When some years later we acquired a battery-run radio and our parents insisted on listening to opera programs, Sonia and I made fun of them for being so old-fashioned. There was all this wonderful music of the day and they listened to that old stuff.

Whenever there was an opportunity for conversation, the subject of farm economics was sure to come up. Everyone was constantly thinking about a way to maximize the return on the effort. On one occasion, our neighbor Manuel Amster put forth that he had done a cost accounting on the profitability of raising chickens and found that it does not pay to raise chickens. A hot argument ensued. Everyone else agreed that raising chickens had been the most dependable source of income, and very often the only one, so how could he come to such a conclusion? It went on for quite a while, Amster showing his figures and the rest treating him as if he had lost his mind.

Eventually my mother changed the drift of the argument by asserting that Amster was right; it does not pay to raise chickens and they should all give it up, provided, of course, that Amster comes up with a product that his research finds profitable. Raising chickens was never challenged again. At that time chickens were not mass-produced anywhere that affected us. Chicken meat was considered special. It had high market value. A farmer didn't butcher a chicken for his own use without giving it much thought. It was said that if you saw a farmer eat a chicken, you could be sure that one or the other was sick.

4. SCHOOL AWAY FROM HOME

On my tenth birthday I was installed in the home of the Folman family in Alcaraz, where I was to live for the duration of the school year. That marked the beginning of a long series of homes I was to live in for the next nine years, in various towns and cities.

The Folman family, like most of the successive ones, took in boarders for economic reasons. Several of the families were headed by widows, but the Folmans were a couple with three children. They treated me the same way they treated their own children. I do not recall feeling especially fond of any of them. I cannot remember what Mr. Folman did for a living. I have a recollection of a quiet man, a hardly noticeable presence.

Mrs. Folman was vivacious and, I presume, considerably younger than her husband. She ran the house doing all the usual things housewives did there in those days. The kids were part of those chores. One of the peculiar things about that household was the sleeping arrangement. Mrs. Folman, her daughter and I slept in one room and Mr. Folman and the two sons in another. At the time I did not think it was strange.

How much supervision I received, I do not remember, but it must have been sufficient, because I cannot recall feeling neglected or afraid. I was lonely sometimes. I missed home. I saw my parents occasionally, once or twice a month. School was six days a week. Although I was only nine miles from home, I could not get there and back in one day. Even when there was a holiday and I had two or three days, it was a problem. My parents had to make two round trips.

Don Francisco did not make that trip. His only mode of transportation was on horseback, and by then the 18 miles round trip was too much for him. I cannot recall his ever riding in the sulky. I now wonder why that was so. It is likely to have been one of Don Francisco's many idiosyncrasies.

Occasionally, my Uncle Abraham whose farm was two or three miles from Alcaraz would come and get me on Saturday for an overnight visit with him, Aunt Peshe and one-year-old Benito. It was a big sacrifice to take all that time off from the endless chores he needed to do. They were poor, struggling without any help, but very kind.

The school in Alcaraz was much larger than in the colony and each class had its own classroom and its own teacher. There was more than one class per grade. There was even a principal. My classmates were more varied. One of my classmates, Montenegro, was one of twenty-five children in his family. Most of them were in that school. He was tall, as if fully grown. He told us that his father had three wives.

Although there were only four grades, the age range was wider because schools in the whole region were a recent development. The law mandated to enroll all children aged six to fourteen. But many of the children did not have any proof of age. Teachers registered the children with whatever names and ages the parents told them. Sometimes they improvised or embellished. My name was Enia. My teacher decided that it was a nickname, short for Eugenia. So my name became Eugenia until a few years later, when I needed to present documents, it went back to Enia.

The village of Alcaraz was the commercial center of our colony. I would often see people I knew who were there on business and to buy provisions. Saturdays and Sundays were very quiet. No farmers, only the few residents remained there. Saturday was a school day. Sunday was the only free day. There was no entertainment of any kind, not even books to read. There was no library in the community or the school. And there was no Don Francisco to amuse the children with stories and games.

Eventually, a girl befriended me during that school year. She was the daughter of Mr. Sepliarsky, the local ICA administrator of our colony. I started spending all my free time at her house. She was an only child and her family lived in a great big house built around an atrium full of exotic plants. The centerpiece was a date palm. I was dazzled by it all. There were servants and things to play with. The fact that the ICA, to my people, represented the enemy didn't seem to bother me. To me, Mr. and Mrs. Sepliarsky were kind people. I felt welcome in their home.

There was a non-Jewish German family in town that I knew from visits with my parents. Their name was Brandauer. Mr. Brandauer repaired agricultural machinery. The entire Jewish colony used his services. He had a large shop and next to it was the home in which he and his family lived. He had a wife and three children. Sometimes when my father brought something to repair, my mother, Sonia and I would come along. While the men discussed business, the women visited and the children played with each other. The eldest of the Brandauer children was a girl near my age. When I was living in Alcaraz I played with her occasionally.

Her mother was a kind person. She was a great gardener. Her flower garden was much admired. She shared her cuttings with anyone who wanted some. Many of the plants in my mother's flower garden originated in Mrs. Brandauer's garden. One day Mrs. Brandauer and her youngest child left to visit family in Germany. Sometime later they returned, and we heard that Mrs. Brandauer was determined to move back to Germany. Germany was now prosperous and a good place to live, she reported. Mr. Brandauer put up a struggle, but she prevailed. They liquidated their possessions and left, never to be heard from again. It was about 1937.

The Folmans' closest friends were the Leibovich family. Mr. Leibovich had a car. That was a mark of great distinction. He was a gregarious fellow and enjoyed giving rides to the kids. At that time, in the whole village, there may have been three or four cars. And I got to ride in one! Years later, I was told that Mrs. Folman was having an affair with Mr. Leibovich during the time I lived in the Folmans' house.

I finished the fourth grade, and there was no fifth grade in Alcaraz. The closest town with a fifth grade was Hasenkamp. From my home Hasenkamp was in the other direction from Alcaraz. It was further away, and there was not a direct road to get there. Either you made a large circle using the existing roads or you took the shorter way crossing fields and trails through woods.

The main road that connected all these towns to the provincial capital, Parana, was about five miles from our farm. This was the only government-maintained road. It was a dirt road made "abovedado" (vaulted). The road was kept rounded for the rain to run off to minimize rutting. A daily bus ran connecting a string of towns to Parana, provided it was not raining. If it started to rain, the bus would have to stop wherever it happened to be and wait until the rain stopped and the road was dry.

Hasenkamp was outside the orbit of the colonies, except for one very important feature. It had a doctor. Dr. Braje was the closest doctor to us. Alcaraz eventually had a doctor, but for a number of years, reaching Dr. Braje in time was often a question of life and death. Nobody with appendicitis survived. The closest hospital was in Parana.

Dr. Braje would make a magnificent subject for an epic film. There were innumerable stories of his benevolence and heroism. Being the only physician in a radius of thirty miles or more, he ministered to everyone who showed up at his door at any hour, often without a cent to pay. When he got paid, it was likely to be a chicken, eggs or some other product the patient produced. Money was not the main currency. Dr. Braje continued practicing in this fashion for years. Then, his son became a doctor and joined him in the practice. Before long the younger Dr. Braje established a modern clinic with regular office hours and money for currency. But by then times had changed. There were other doctors, and there were small hospitals that the government or missionaries established. That was long after we had left.

My parents took me to Hasenkamp to enroll me in the fifth grade and to find a boarding home or "pension," as we called it. Abraham Berdichevsky's and Lina Sandomirsky's parents brought them to do the same. Lina was to stay with the Jewish family that owned the dry goods store. Abraham and I ended up nearby with the Fernandez family. It was a new experience. The family was from the province of Tucuman in the far northwest of Argentina and they were Catholics. Abraham, Lina and I knew each other from the school in the colony. Our parents knew each other socially. We were in the same grade.

The Fernandez family consisted of four adults—a widowed mother, two grown sons and a grown daughter. The older son was the only employed person in the family. He worked for the railroad and was away much of the time. I shared a bedroom with the mother and daughter. Abraham shared a bedroom with the sons. Mrs. Fernandez was an excellent cook. During a recent visit with Abraham while reminiscing about that period, we dwelt on the great meals Mrs. Fernandez served. He reminded me of the delicious "locro," a corn and meat stew of Quechua origin. She also made a variety of tasty pasta dishes. Sunday dinner always included homemade tallarines.

Abraham and I became devoted friends. We looked out for each other. We did not know anyone in town, and no one we knew came there. Lina was in a home with two young girls and apparently well occupied. Abraham and I spent our free time together. Although we felt fairly treated, we must have had some reservations about how much we could impose on the family. That would explain the following episode.

Early one morning, I woke up with a very sore throat. I looked at my throat in the mirror and saw that it was all white. The next thing I remember is that I was on the way to see Dr. Braje accompanied by Abraham. I was eleven and Abraham was a year younger. Dr. Braje told me that I had an advanced case of diphtheria and he was going to give me a large dose of serum, which might give me some side effects, but there was no other choice.

Done with the doctor, we went home. It was decided that I was going home to my parents. The only bus that came through town would take me within five miles of my parents. It passed through town in late afternoon. I was taking a chance that from where the bus left me off a farmer might be passing by and give me a ride, at least to my aunt's house. And so I boarded a bus packed with people, and, as it was winter, all the windows were closed. That is how I set off for home.

When I got off it was already dusk. I started walking. After a while someone in a wagon came along and gave me a ride to my aunt's house. The only one home was my cousin Marcos, who was fourteen at the time. I wanted to reach home. He was at a loss of what to do because there were no horses nearby. It was already dark and going for horses in the far fields was not a good idea. So he walked me home. I arrived home and gave my parents a terrible fright. I was feverish and looked ghastly.

I remember the relief I felt from having made it home. The responsibility of achieving the goal was over. Now all I had to do was to get well. I don't recall worrying about that. I felt safe in the care of my parents. I also didn't know anything about the seriousness of diphtheria. The epidemic was just starting. I guess I must have been warned not to talk about it. Getting on that bus must have given the epidemic a big boost.

When I got back to Hasenkamp, I found out that a school officer had been to inquire about the case of diphtheria. I do not remember whether Abraham was kept out of school. I know that he did not get the disease. I went back to school and, within a day or two, came down with a case of hives and inability to move my legs. Dr. Braje diagnosed it as the side effect of that large dose of serum. Not to worry; it will go away. I had no alternative to staying put. It did disappear in a few days. It must have been incredibly difficult for my parents to send me away to school under such circumstances. They really felt they had no choice. The consequences of not sending me away were unthinkable.

During the time I lived with the Fernandez family, I never thought they were peculiar, except for their sing-song speech. They were the only people from Tucuman I had ever met. The fact that a mother and two grown siblings moved around the country with the sole working member of the family didn't seem odd to me. I learned years later from Abraham that the non-working son suffered from leprosy and died of it not long after.

The school in Alcaraz had expanded, and now I was back in Alcaraz. This time I lived with the Slavins, a recently married young couple. I shared a room with a young teacher, Miss Franchini, who had come from Parana to teach. A rural school was the first post for any teacher who wanted to enter the system.

I have fond memories of that year. I liked Miss Franchini. She talked about life in the big city and the big world out there. She told me her sad story, which fascinated me. She had had a handsome boyfriend for years, and they were preparing to get married when he came down with appendicitis and died in the hospital after the operation. Now she was never going to date, because that was the love of her life. God had meant for her to do something else with her life. I thought that was so romantic. I admired her.

Exposure to the non-Jewish world, which was entirely Catholic, was a new experience. The non-Jews in the colonies, with the exception of my teacher Mrs. Bertozzi and her family, were mainly illiterate natives of the region. The police chief could not read or write. He had a semi-literate clerk who did the paper work, such as it was. The population was nominally Catholic. Every five years or so a priest would come through to baptize people. There wasn't a church anywhere in the district. We never heard of gentiles being anything other than Catholic. Eventually, after we had left, missionaries of several denominations arrived and established churches, hospitals and other social services throughout the region. Non-Catholics all taken together are a small minority to this day. Until 1996, only a Catholic could be president, and the president was the country's highest representative of the Pope.

The Fernandez family and Miss Franchini introduced me to some of the customs. I learned about "luto," the wearing of black as a sign of mourning for a dead relative. Mrs. Fernandez, being a widow, wore only black. That was for the rest of her life. Miss Franchini, not having been married to the man who died, did not wear black, but otherwise acted the part of the widow. She didn't attend any festivities, as custom dictates for those in mourning. These customs came from Spain. However, people from other backgrounds, including many Jews, adopted them. The Jews in the colonies were the exception. Their insulation created conditions for a particular culture to emerge. The blending of customs of Jews from many lands and diverse backgrounds, with the admixture influence of the indigenous population resulted in a unique specimen, the Jewish gaucho.

Mr. Slavin was the *gerente* (manager) of the farmers' cooperative. Mrs. Slavin ran the household efficiently. She was a good cook and knew how to sew, knit and embroider. She knew how to do everything that made young women into admirable homemakers. The Slavin home was warm and pleasant.

Mrs. Slavin was pregnant at the time I arrived. One Sunday morning, when I woke up, I found out that during the night Mrs. Slavin had given birth to a little boy. Mr. Slavin expressed his amazement at my sleeping through all the commotion and noise. He asked me to cook a chicken Mrs. Slavin had prepared for the noon dinner. I had never cooked a chicken, but I did not say so. I just went ahead with the task. I remember the teasing I took about the delicious chicken floating in oil.

At that time, Alcaraz was at its peak of development. It had two large general stores; one was Libedinsky's, owned by a family man; the other was Serebrinsky's, owned by a bachelor.

Bernardo Serebrinsky was a notorious ladies' man. He had arrived in Alcaraz from Parana with a far and wide reputation as a Casanova. He had only one lung. An enraged husband shot him when he found him in bed with his wife. It cost him a lung. In Alcaraz, he managed to avoid enraged husbands. On any day that one went to his store there were swarms of children who claimed to be Bernardo's sons and daughters. Bernardo Serebrinsky was a personable fellow. He was a town character, and he enjoyed his reputation.

The farmers' cooperative, *Cooperativa Agricola Ocavi Ltda,* ran a large general store, besides being the agent for selling the agricultural products of the colony. The machine repair shop that had belonged to Brandauer was now owned and operated by Bernardo Keilin, the son of a farmer in the colony. There was a doctor in town and also a pharmacy. The pharmacist was Miss Saslavsky, a sister of Mrs. Slavin. A dentist came one day every two weeks, mostly to pull teeth. There were a number of small shops called *boliches.* They sold liquor, food and other items. We had a couple of barbers (unisex), dressmakers, a shoe repairman and other craftsmen.

There was something akin to a pool hall, where men drank and played games. These served mostly the indigenous population and were frequently the sites of knifings. All indigenous men carried knives, which mixed with a few alcoholic drinks, resulted in duels. The railroad station had a telegraph and the only telephone in town. The power plant worked evenings for three hours. Electricity was used for lights only. Nowhere around was there a church or synagogue or any other public building with the exception of schools. There were no paved streets. Any social function was held outdoors on any empty space available.

The school in Alcaraz was still missing the last elementary grade. The principal of the school offered, for a fee, to prepare a group of students in the summer for a test to make the grade. Parents who were going to send their children away to school were happy to take the offer. I think there were five or six of us in the class. A couple of others and I stayed in Alcaraz, and some were commuters. We went to class and cheerfully studied whatever we were assigned. At the end of the summer three of us were told that we had to go to La Paz for the test, and the others were to go to another place. La Paz was a city outside our orbit, but reachable by train. The principal was no longer involved. My mother took upon herself to make the arrangements for our group and to accompany us. The Fernandez family, in whose home Abraham Berdichevsky and I had once lived, was now living in La Paz. My mother contacted them for accommodations, and Mrs. Fernandez was happy to put us all up. Hotels were used only as a last resort.

All went smoothly, except the test. It consisted of three parts given in three sessions. We all passed the first and second, which were math and language. The third was entirely alien to me. I did not know what to do with it. All I remember is the anguish. I can still see my mother's pained face when she learned that I failed. Besides the humiliation, I was overwhelmed by guilt. I recently asked Yacov Klainer, the only one who passed it, to tell me how he did it. It was a multiple-choice world geography test, he explained. None of us had ever seen a multiple-choice test, and the content was not covered in class. He figured out the format, and he knew the answers. He just knew it from general reading, not from class.

The last grade of primary school I did in Parana, the capital city of the province of Entre Rios. Parana sits on the hilly east bank of the Parana River. It was and is a beautiful city. For me it was an incredible experience to arrive in such a grand place. The last time I had seen a city I was six years old. Now I was fourteen.

In Parana, to find lodging for me, my parents consulted Mr. Miller who had left the colony to take a job as sexton in the synagogue-community center there. Mr. Miller knew the entire Jewish community of Parana. He was the colony's sole contact in Parana. Whether illness or other need brought a farmer to Parana, Mr. and Mrs. Miller helped the visitor in every way they could. Generosity came naturally to them, and their deeds were long remembered. Mr. Miller suggested the Goldin family for my lodging. The family consisted of Mrs. Goldin, a widow, and her three grown daughters. They were recent arrivals from a small town. Mrs. Goldin had talked to Mr. Miller about her wishes to get boarders and asked him to send her prospects. That is how I arrived at the Goldins.

The Goldins lived in a nice, attractively furnished house. They had been well off until Mr. Goldin died. He had had a business, which no one knew how to run after his death. It was lost. The family had no future in the small town. There were no jobs for the young women, and Mrs. Goldin had never worked. Besides, she had been accustomed to a life she no longer could afford. Relatives helped them make the move and continued to bail them out frequently.

There were two other people boarding at Mrs. Goldin's. There was a couple who had a large room and took their meals in their room. I don't recall their name or what he looked like. The man was away most of the time--on business, I was told. I remember her vividly. I shall call her Mrs. X. Mrs. X had a telephone, the only one in the house. She allowed the other people in the house to use it. I had never used a telephone. When she was out, the Goldins would answer the phone.

One day when Mrs. X was out, the telephone rang and I was asked to go answer it. I picked up the receiver, and a barrage of talk poured out of it. Totally confused, I asked who was talking and the reply was, "X." I came back with: "Mr. or Mrs.?" At this point Mrs. X lost her temper and amidst the barrage that came over the line, was: "you have to be pretty stupid not to be able to tell a difference between a woman's and man's voice." I don't think I ever touched that phone again. I also didn't get in Mrs. X's way, if at all possible. I didn't miss using a telephone. I did not know anyone to whom I wanted to talk who had a telephone.

One day Mrs. X returned home terribly agitated with the news that friends of hers died in a car mishap. The car, with five people aboard, accidentally ended up in the river and all passengers drowned. When I arrived at school the next morning, everyone was talking about the horrible murder-suicide. The morning paper, which I had not seen, told in detail how and why the tragedy happened. The driver was an older man, and the four passengers were women: A middle aged mother (widow), a daughter in her early twenties and two young friends visiting from out of town. The driver was the mother's lover. He had wanted to marry the daughter and been rebuffed. On the pretext of showing the visitors the town, he got them all into his car and drove into the river. For weeks the papers were full of the story. It was the only subject during school recesses. We debated morality, sin, salvation and all other aspects of the tragedy.

At Mrs. Goldin's, I had a room to myself for the first time. It was in back and probably built as servants' quarters. But it was quite adequate and I was pleased with it. Meals were served in a formal dining room. The eldest daughter was kind and, I thought, not appreciated by her family. The middle daughter had a boyfriend who took his meals there. His name was Toledo and he was a penniless tailor hoping to get his own shop someday. For lack of money, marriage was not imminent. The youngest daughter, I dimly recall, was finishing her baccalaureate or normal school.

In Parana, I went to a girls' school. It was a big school with several classes to a grade. It seemed luxurious to me at the time. There were so many more teaching tools, like maps, books of all kinds, and incredible things like a world globe. And the girls were so sophisticated. They sounded so grownup. Boys and going to confession were the most exciting of subjects -- the ways to fool your parents and the ways to get cleared from sin by the priest. They were not subjects I could participate in. I had to take care of myself and be responsible. I couldn't play those games. And as for priests and confessions, I could hardly believe my ears.

It was in Parana that I saw my first film. I discovered Sunday matinees, which were very cheap and consisted of triple features. I was soon immersed in movie lore. At first I was in awe at all the girls' knowledge about actors and their movies, but, before long, I was participating in movie talk. Going to the movies took care of Sundays. Getting up late, eating Sunday dinner at noon, and going to the movies made for a full day. Some Sundays I dedicated to exploring the city. I walked everywhere, most of the time with someone else.

Abraham Berdichevsky was in Parana, too. He was living with another family and going to a different school, but we saw a lot of each other. He had a sweet disposition and was always willing to go wherever I proposed. There was Parque Urquiza, on the hilly banks of the river. There was also a famous park, the name of which escapes me now, with the most imaginative playground and sports equipment. And there were endless other attractions for someone who had never seen a beautiful building, a large bridge, a public garden or a sculpture in a plaza.

Once Abraham's father came to town and took Abraham and me to an elegant "confiteria" (café-teahouse-bar). He blew us away. The idea that someone from the colony would dare to enter such a place and order all those incredible pastries was overwhelming. Only Abraham's father was capable of it. He liked to make believe that he belonged there. He was not entirely beaten down.

In Parana, I entered the world of modern amenities such as inside plumbing, around the clock electricity, radio and telephones. It was a world so removed from my experience that I needed to find my bearings. But I realized that it was the world my parents, especially my mother, so often spoke about. That is where I was to belong. I felt sorry for my parents who were stuck in that ghastly wilderness without hope of escape. It was 1939, the year World War II broke out.

I don't remember my parents coming to see me during that year. I went home at least once during school break. Once in a while someone from the colony would come to Parana and look me up. In August or September of that year Shloime Stirin, a distant relative who lived in the colony came to see me. I knew him as a bachelor, but he arrived accompanied by a most attractive young woman. He explained that she had just arrived from Poland. She had come to marry him. He had sent for her. They were on their way from Buenos Aires to the farm, and Parana was a stop en route.

I remember feeling sorry for her at first sight. She surely didn't know what she was getting into. Speaking Yiddish, we spent some time together. I realized that was indeed the case. She was totally unprepared, if there is such a thing as preparation for that kind of life. Of course, the war broke out within a month or so, and she was probably the only member of her family to survive. However, her story ended in great tragedy, too. She undertook to make the best of her life in the colony. For a few years she struggled like the rest of the farmers' wives. During those few years, she gave birth to three daughters. Then relatives raised the girls because their mother had gone mad. She has been in a mental institution ever since. Her husband and two daughters died recently, all three in one year. I saw Shifre, the surviving daughter, when I was in Buenos Aires recently. She talked about visiting her mother all those years.

The year in Parana was coming to an end. I was packing to go home, when Mrs. Goldin asked me for the last monthly board payment. I was shocked. I knew my parents had been paying in advance and that they had made the last payment and I told her so. She left and didn't pursue the matter any further. But Toledo, the future son-in-law, that evening, came to me and gave me a mean-spirited sermon about taking advantage of a widow. I had visions of my parents having to prove without receipts that they had paid in full. Mrs. Goldin never gave receipts. All the payments were made in cash. Banks were unknown to farmers. No one in that world had any money to put in a bank. The only time the word bank was mentioned was when, after a major disaster, the farmers were unable to buy seed for planting the next harvest. Then the ICA and the government would step in to guarantee loans to the farmers.

We never heard about the matter again. What we did hear was that Toledo had won ten thousand pesos in the lottery, had opened his own tailor shop and gotten married to the Goldin young woman. Sometime later, my parents received a letter from Toledo advising them that he was planning to visit the colony on business. He was coming to take orders for suits. He hoped that my father would take advantage of the opportunity. My father did. That was the only suit he acquired during the fifteen years we lived in Argentina. It was the suit in which he arrived in the United States.

I was now finished with elementary school. I came home to spend the summer as I had done every year. I had a difficult decision to make. Where was I to go next? There were four kinds of secondary schools. Normal schools offered four-year courses with a degree in education. Commercial schools offered five-year courses with a degree in accounting. Industrial schools offered six-year courses with an engineering degree. And lyceums offered five-year courses with a general baccalaureate degree.

Parana had a normal school and a lyceum. Teaching was not practical because new teachers had to serve for the first five or more years in rural areas. Besides, elementary school teaching held no special attraction for me. And a general baccalaureate was impractical because it would not give me a way to earn money. I would need to be self-sufficient at that point. My sister Sonia had been boarding already in Alcaraz and would be ready soon to go away to a city.

The industrial school would have been the best choice for me given my aptitude and circumstances. Mathematics was what I liked and excelled in. But the industrial school did not accept women. I was left with the commercial school as the only choice. It meant going to Buenos Aires. What a jump. Where would I stay? And that year the harvest failed completely. There was no money at all. We did not consider the possibility that I might not get in. That did not occur to us. We had no idea that in Buenos Aires the commercial school admitted only twelve percent of those who took the entrance exam and that there were special courses to prepare for it.

The sacrifices that my parents made to send us away still haunt me. They had both of us away. They missed us and worried about our safety. And the worst of it was the constant worry about having the money to pay for it. My mother wrote to her siblings in the United States to ask for help. Uncle Sam, who was in dire financial straits himself, managed to send some money at critical times, undoubtedly with Uncle Willie's help. My parents who were such proud people were now reduced to asking for help everywhere.

Aunt Leike had been sending packages of clothing to us and to the Penchanskys since the beginning. It must have been her full-time occupation collecting the clothes from dozens of relatives, packaging it, making out the customs forms and mailing it. But those packages were manna in the wilderness to us. They were our main source of clothing. Aunt Leike was our fairy godmother.

I remember the summer that I was to enter secondary school as the gloomiest of the many gloomy summers I experienced in the colony. I cannot recall the circumstances that caused the total failure of the harvest. I only recall the sadness that engulfed the community. I was embarrassed to talk about going away to school. Sonia and I were considered rich girls, indulged and spoiled. And by those standards one can understand why. My parents were going through a double crisis. They had the same problem as the rest of the farmers of having lost everything they had put into the harvest, and besides, they had the problem of financing their daughters' education. They never talked about the latter. It was insensitive to mention such a luxury as sending children away to school when the question of survival was the subject. A failed harvest meant debts could not be paid and there was no seed for planting next year's harvest. And, to complete the aura of imminent doom, the war in Europe was raging and the Nazis were winning. Everybody in the colony had family in the war's path.

My parents must have been talking about what to do about me, because I overheard my mother saying to my father: "you must write to Tsile, she is our last resort." I did not know who Tsile was. I asked my mother who Tsile was and was told she was my father's cousin who lived in Buenos Aires. My father obviously wrote because, within a few weeks, I was told that I was going to Buenos Aires to take the entrance exam at the commercial school.

Father took me to Buenos Aires. Although he tried to keep it from me, I was much aware of how low he felt. It was a long trip in those days, by buggy to Alcaraz, by train to Parana, a bus from the train station to the port, a ferry across the Parana River to Santa Fe, a bus from the port to the railroad station, and finally an overnight train to Buenos Aires. Although my father was usually a man of few words, he talked at length about a number of subjects, as if trying to dispel our uneasiness. He gave me advice about safety in a big city and about making friends wisely. And, as for young men, "be careful, you must not trust them, or yourself around them." There was no advice about studying. There had never been any. It was so clearly understood that it was unnecessary to talk about it.

We arrived in Retiro, the central railroad station of Buenos Aires. From Retiro the rails fan out to the whole country. It is enormous and intimidating. We made our way out and inquired about public transportation to the address we had. We took a subway that took us to the station we were told to get off. When we got off, we asked for directions, but got lost following them. I remember my father feeling sorry for me schlepping heavy packages. He was disheartened about the whole enterprise of bringing me to a cousin whose husband he had never met, probably feeling that she may have not been able to refuse. My parents spared me any details of their discomforts in relation to my going there, but I felt their tension and sadness. We finally arrived at the grocery store of Gregorio and Tsile Krusinski where we were warmly received by them and their nine-year-old daughter Raquel.

The living quarters were in back of the store. They put us up in the large room which was a dining-living room combination. The Krusinskis worked long hours seven days a week. All the conversation took place in the store. Father stayed a couple of days during which we visited Jacobo and Ines Penchansky and their son Manuel who was about two years old. As I recall we had a pleasant visit, but many years later I found out that my father thought otherwise. He remembered being slighted by Ines.

When father left, I dedicated myself to the task of applying for the entrance exam to the commercial school. I found out the school's name: Escuela Nacional Superior de Comercio Antonio Bermejo. It was located on Avenida Callao in the congested center of the city. I had no experience in crossing such streets. On one of my early trips downtown, a woman grabbed me to get me out of the path of oncoming traffic. She undoubtedly saved my life. She also explained to me how to cross a street safely. There were some required papers to obtain; one was the *cedula de identidad* which everyone above a certain age needed to carry for identification purposes. The *cedula*, I was told could not be ready by the date the school application was to be submitted. I went home and told my predicament to Tsile and Gregorio. They told me not to worry. Someone in the family knew a politician that could fix it. And, if that did not work, there was always the bribe method. For such a minor thing, it would not be more than a few pesos. I was greatly relieved when I learned that the politician fixed it.

Enia at school – 1940

I took the exam, which consisted of two parts, Spanish and mathematics. I was sure that I had done very well in the math part, at which I knew I was proficient, but I was not as confident about the Spanish part. A week or so later I was notified that I was admitted. The news of my success was greeted with shock and disbelief. Apparently I had been the laughing stock of the relatives and friends of the Krusinskis and maybe of the Krusinskis themselves. The idea of bringing a country youngster to Buenos Aires and assuming that she would get admitted to Antonio Bermejo, when some of their children failed to do it, they considered incredible chutzpa.

Raquel and I spent much of our time together. Her parents were always at work and, I assume she was with them in the store when I was not there. I do not remember family meals. Tsile would appear in the kitchen to fix food and serve Raquel and me. I had no friends for quite a while. My schoolmates lived in other neighborhoods. Eventually I made friends with girls who took me home to study together or play. I never brought anyone home.

On Sundays I often went to visit Jacobo and his family. I felt comfortable with them, especially with Jacobo. I played with little Manuel. They took me to two incredibly sumptuous weddings of Ines's rich relatives. In those days it was the custom to welcome invited guests to bring extra young people to weddings. They were called *colados* (tailers). Eventually, sophistication arrived, and the custom was abandoned. Another custom was to pay for a spread of photographs of the wedding in the Jewish paper. Some would occupy the double-page center of the paper. That is how one learned who was who among the rich. The two weddings that I attended were admirable charity fundraisers. In lieu of gifts to the couple, they asked for money for the Zionist cause. I found it hard to believe how large the sums they raised were.

I tried to help Tsile with housework whenever I could. I stocked the empty boxes that were scattered in the patio and cleaned it, improving its appearance considerably, I thought. The patio was at the entrance to the living quarters, and it was usually littered with refuse from the store. The Krusinskis thought it was funny that I bothered cleaning it up over and over again. I thought they were peculiar not to care, not to appreciate the difference.

Tsile was one of three sisters who had come, one at a time, to Argentina in the nineteen thirties. Their eldest sister had gone to the United States. The rest of the large family remained in Europe and perished in the Holocaust. Tsile married Gregorio Krusinsky who had come earlier from the same area in then Poland. Gregorio was a recent widower and had a baby daughter, Raquel. Raquel's mother had died of breast cancer.

Tsile was a devoted mother to Raquel. She adored the child. But she also was desperate to give birth to a child. By the time I came to live there, she had been trying for a number of years. She had miscarriages and other problems, but she never gave up. Four years after I left, and after more than ten years of trying, Tsile was rewarded with a healthy, beautiful girl whom they named Betty. They had sold the grocery store and were living more comfortably in pleasant surroundings. Raquel grew up and, got married and had a son. She came down with breast cancer and died of it, just as her biological mother did. Tsile undertook to raise the little boy. Later when his father remarried, he took the boy.

I recently reconnected with Betty who married Rafael Berdichevsky, a younger brother of my old friend Abraham. It was such a touching experience. Betty married very young without finishing her education and to a farmer. It caused her parents much pain. Rafael is now a successful businessman and a gentleman farmer. Betty went back to school and became a psychologist. It is sad that her parents did not live to see it. Having been born so late in her parents' lives, she knew very little about them. She wanted to know everything I could tell her.

Betty and Rafael live in Parana. They have three married children. Only one of them, a son, lives in Parana. Two of their children, a son and a daughter, went to university in Israel. Both graduated from the Technion. The daughter settled in Israel. The son works for an international enterprise and lives in different countries. Rafael is studying English in fear that he may find himself not being able to speak with his grandchildren who live abroad, unless he equips himself with more languages. Hebrew he knows from childhood. His parents were Palestinian Jews who continued to speak Hebrew at home. Betty and Rafael are enthusiastic travelers. Betty has recently located the son of her dead sister Raquel. They visited him in Mexico where he now lives.

The big event of that school year that I spent at the Krusinskys was the birth of my sister Ines. I learned that my mother was pregnant shortly before the event. I bought wool yarn and knitted as fast as I could a sweater to be ready when she was born. I sent it off proud of my accomplishment. It fit her only for a couple of weeks, I later found out. She was a big baby. Ines changed the situation at home. Now my parents had a child at home to fill the void left by the children who were away. Don Francisco had a full-time occupation watching over her.

Following Ines's arrival, my parents' letters to me were more cheerful, even though nothing otherwise had changed. The same problems continued to plague the colony, but there was this child to hold and love. I met Ines when she was two months old, when I came home for summer vacation. Sonia and I lavished a lot of attention on our little sister. I was fifteen and Sonia was eleven. It was a different household, all revolving about this little girl.

We had no camera to document events. Once Aunt Leike sent us a Brownie from the United States. It came with a roll of film, which we used up learning how to do it. Eventually, when we had the film developed, we found out how poorly we had focused. I don't know what happened to the camera. Maybe we just never got more film. Sometime during that year in Buenos Aires, someone took a photograph of me and I sent it home. It was later related to me that my mother burst out crying when she saw it. I looked like a waif in it, she said. Maybe it was just as well not to have the visual documentation of the period.

Summers when I was home, I saw my old friends, especially the Penchansky kids. There was also Lina Sandomirsky whose family had moved away from the colony to a small town called El Cimarron. El Cimarron was a town even smaller than Alcaraz, and had no colonies surrounding it. Her parents had a small general store there. It was an escape from the colony. Lina was sent away to school to Concordia, a city on the banks of the Uruguay River. The significant advantage of living in a town over living on a farm was that all these towns were along a railroad line connecting Parana, the provincial capital, to Concordia, the second largest city. Rain or mud did not interfere with travel.

The Sandomirsky family lived an isolated existence there, but they did not have the ICA to deal with, and their livelihood was easier and more secure. During summer vacations Lina would come to visit her grandmother and assorted aunts and uncles still living in the colony and see her old friends. Her bachelor uncle Yanie married my father's cousin Rohel, a widow. Lina's grandmother lived with them. After a few years we became related to many families. The marriages tended to be between families of the same area in Europe. Much was made of the differences between Litvaks and Galitzianers, and later even more of Yekes (German Jews) when they arrived. In some cases, we became related several ways.

My father's brother married a distant relative of my mother. Among my Argentine relatives I am often related independently to each member of a couple. The isolation of the colony was such that there was hardly contact with the world outside. As hope for a better life dimmed, young people started to leave, almost always never to come back. Eventually all hope died and the exodus of the young was almost complete.

Saturdays the teenagers would gather in the schoolhouse to socialize. We planned programs that we could carry out with our meager resources. If we could find someone who had a wind-up record player and records, willing to lend them to us, we would have a dance or a musicale, depending on the type of records. When we were especially ambitious we would undertake a big project such as a kermess, a fund-raiser for some charity. On occasion we would organize the group to go to a fiesta of some sort held elsewhere within a buggy-ride distance. It could not be on a moonless night because it was impossible to ride in total darkness.

In our colony, my generation was the first not to have had any European experience. We had come too young to have learned things such as theater or music. The older generation had members who had been actors or musicians. They were able to produce plays or other performances. We were the most avid members of the audience. Besides reading, it was the only thing we had that gave us a taste of what culture out there in the world was. And access to books was limited to the twenty or thirty books per year bought for our community library. The Yiddish paper from Buenos Aires was the only source of news of the world. My parents also regularly received the *Forverts* from the United States, courtesy of Aunt Leike.

In the late nineteen thirties, just before the Second World War broke out, a number of German-Jewish families arrived to settle in the colony. They came from cities and were worldlier in education and culture than the original colonists. They knew even such things as vaudeville and burlesque. One summer after their arrival, we were planning a kermess. It was to be held outdoors in the daytime at an old *estancia* (ranch). Its extensive grounds had beautiful shade trees, which made it a good place for gatherings. Whole families came to such events.

At a planning meeting one of the recent arrivals, a young man, offered that he could get a group of fellows to do a take-off on the Andrews Sisters. We had no idea what that was, but from his description it sounded like fun and we were all for it. The performance turned out to be quite spectacular. A chorus line of about ten young men dressed in women's cabaret-type costumes, all the necessary padding and tresses added, danced and sang along a recording of the Andrews Sisters.

The crowd watched as in a trance. They were stunned by its boldness. Everyone turned a critic. Some pointed out that it was not fit for children. Some said it offended their sense of propriety. Others thought it was a superb performance, although a bit too risqué. It provided a subject for discussion for the rest of the summer.

Notwithstanding the closed community in which I spent my first years in Argentina, acculturation to the larger environment was swift. I learned to sew, embroider, and knit from the first grade on, all things my mother never did. I never missed an opportunity to learn something. We did not have a sewing machine, but I learned to sew and borrowed one wherever I could. When I was eleven and was in Hasenkamp, I took pattern-making classes. It was a practical thing to do, but more than that, it was what girls did.

Embroidering was not practical and I was not good at it, but I felt the need to prove that I could do it. There exists, as a reminder of our labors, a garishly embroidered tablecloth that Sonia and I made. Later when we were grown and in the US, we argued about who should have it. I lost the argument and got the tablecloth. I spent my summers helping with the work around the house. Sewing came in very handy. The clothes that Aunt Leike sent us needed adjusting or altering and I could do much of it. She also sent us cloth from which I sewed new garments. In fact, when already in the United States, I found it useful in the early years of my marriage. I made clothes for my children when I could not afford the clothes I wanted them to have. I still have a sewing machine, which I occasionally use for minor repairs or to make pillows for my grandchildren or clothes for their dolls.

The next year in Buenos Aires I lived with the Rubinson Family. After the death of Uri Rubinson, my Jewish teacher in the colony, his family moved to Buenos Aires. The family consisted of the widow, Rhoda, two sons, Leiser and Hillel, and a daughter, Rivka. Hillel was in his late teens and Leiser in his early twenties. Rivka was ten years old. The boys were studying at the university. Hillel was also working full time. They rented three rooms and a shared kitchen in a big house in central Buenos Aires. Two of the rooms were on the first floor; one served as the dining room, study room and living room, and the other was the bedroom for Mrs. Rubinson, Rivka and me. The boys' bedroom was upstairs. The kitchen was on the first floor in the back. The bathroom was also in the rear. Although now this seems less than adequate, it was quite all right then.

The entire experience turned out most satisfactorily. It was the best of my lodging years while in school. I was with people who had much to offer intellectually. That home was a place where serious conversation was fun. I had for the most part been living devoid of any intellectual stimulation, but for that which I would seek on my own outside. While I tried to go to museums and attend cultural events whenever I could, I had nobody to talk to about it when I got home. At the Rubinsons everyone was interested and ready to discuss any subject. It was also a place I could invite a friend to drop in.

It was 1941 and most of my Penchansky cousins were in Buenos Aires and some of my colony friends too. They all worked. Some also went to school at night, or worked at night and went to school by day. Those were desperate times for the young people of the colony. With every passing year hope of improvement diminished, until none was left. The ICA did absolutely nothing to improve the situation. The local administrators now had a ready excuse. It was wartime, and the ICA central administration was in exile and could not take any action. It didn't make sense to us then and doesn't to me now. The commitment to the status quo was unshakable until Peron shook it, some years later. It is the height of irony that Peron would be the rescuer of the Jewish colonists from their Jewish oppressors.

The next year I transferred to the commercial school of La Plata. My father's cousin Libe lived in La Plata. She was Tsile's sister and had met me when I lived at Tsile's. I do not recall the particular circumstances that triggered that decision for the change, but, there I was, moving once again. This time it was a radical change. La Plata, the capital of the province of Buenos Aires, is a planned city. Buenos Aires, the capital of the country, was in the province of the same name and also the seat of the provincial government. When a federal district was created for the national capital, a new city, La Plata, was created to be the capital of the Province of Buenos Aires. The location picked was about thirty miles from Buenos Aires. As Buenos Aires grew to be a very large city, La Plata became part of the ring of its outer suburbs. Because it was a planned city, La Plata has a thoroughly logical grid of streets and diagonal avenues. Plazas, parks and other amenities were included in the original design. It was a sleepy government and university town. The only remarkable institution that I recall is a world class museum of natural history.

I spent three years in La Plata living at the home of the Novomisky family, Libe and Mauricio and their children Marcos and Dorita. They had a modern apartment in back of their jeans workshop. They made a living manufacturing jeans, which at that time were strictly working clothes. In the shop, they cut the cloth and prepared the bundles to be picked up by seamstresses who worked at home. It was a small wholesale business. The location was a far distance from the center of the city in a quiet working class neighborhood. No one I met at school lived nearby. I went by streetcar to school and anywhere else I needed or wanted to go. Most of my activities were immediately before or after school in order to save time and money. I seldom ventured out by myself after dark.

Libe was a caring person and I was most appreciative of her kindness. She had a hard life, but remained cheerful and kept hope alive. She never complained. Mauricio, although he seemed to love his family, was not easy to live with. He was a frustrated man. To him the world was organized to thwart his ambitions. Libe and I had a warm relationship. I also got along well with Mauricio. I had learned, in all those years living in other people's homes, how to get along with all kinds of people.

Marcos was four years younger than I was and fully absorbed in sports. He had a real problem with being Jewish. Living in an entirely non-Jewish environment, he ran into a lot of anti-Semitism. There were no Jewish children to serve as a countervailing force to this predicament. The only way he found to survive in such an environment was to try to pass. That meant not to be seen with his parents. One of the biggest surprises in my life was to learn that Marcos' children, after finishing university, went to live in Israel. Dorita was under ten when I lived with the Novomiskys. I found her a delightful child, a free spirit, always ready to have fun. I liked to play with her.

Sonia and Enia at the farm 1942

School in La Plata was more intimate than in Buenos Aires. The students got to know each other. There were organized activities such as outings in the country, attending cultural events and even trips to Buenos Aires. That was my main social life in La Plata. For a long time I was under the impression that I was the only Jew in my class. Those were the years of World War II, and Argentina was sympathetic to the Nazis. It was not a comfortable situation for Jews to live in a country that obviously was on the side of the Jews' archenemy.

I did not suffer from anti-Semitism per se, but what went with it. Suddenly, attending Catholic services at church was mandated on specific occasions. Non-Catholics could opt to sit outside the church while the classmates were attending services. I remember doing just that by myself. Later when a girl classmate's father died, it became clear that she was Jewish. Then, another girl told that she too was Jewish. They must have skipped class the day I sat alone outside the church. They were both Sephardic with non-suspect names.

I discovered a number of resources that gave an outlet to my desire to do things, experience the world. There was a great library in La Plata and I became a regular there. Libe was happy when I followed her advice and brought home a book by a Russian master. Sometimes she recited Russian poetry to me. I felt sorry not to understand it, but I listened. Across the street from my school stood the building of the City's major newspaper. I found out that they had tickets to movie theaters that they sold at a considerable discount. I became a regular moviegoer; sometimes even cutting classes to see a "must" film. My favorites at the time were ballet films. I usually found a girl classmate to go along. Casual dating was just not done. Going out with a boy was a serious matter. I did go to a Jewish youth club occasionally. Libe or Mauricio would pick me up because they did not think it was safe to come home alone, and nobody lived near me.

Once I was asked to take a part in a Yiddish play. They needed a young woman and had trouble finding someone young who spoke the language. I remember going to rehearsals and being annoyed at the lack of seriousness displayed by my fellow actors. They did not show proper respect; they arrived late, took directions casually, and, in general did not take it seriously, as I thought we should. The director and his wife were professional actors and worked hard to produce the show. To my surprise, it turned out well, but I decided not to be part of the group. That was a very foolish decision. It was an opportunity to learn something that interested me. I loved theater from the first time I saw a production in the colony. On occasion I attended professional theater while I lived in Buenos Aires. They were the highlights of my life there. Here I had an opportunity to be taught by professionals, and I did not take it. Not long after, the director and his wife emigrated to the United States to work in the Yiddish theater.

74

In La Plata I was in exile. Whenever I could, which was not very often, I took the train to Buenos Aires to see relatives and friends there. My cousin Yenie, her husband Zev and their daughters Ester and Yudit had moved to Buenos Aires. Zev and Yenie bought a grocery store in which they both worked. Their living quarters were attached to the store. It was an apartment just adequate for the four of them. Nechama, who was attending Jewish seminary, was living with them.

In their home there was always room for me. I did not need to ask, just as I had not needed to ask in Aunt Feigl's home. Five of the seven Penchanskys of my generation were living in Buenos Aires. As the colony was emptying of youth, Buenos Aires was becoming populated with the exiles. Nobody came to La Plata. The only exception was Leiser Rubinson, who was studying law at the La Plata University Law School. It must have been a special program, because he only attended occasionally. He came to visit me. Libe always made sure he left well fed. I am sure that kept him coming.

In November 1943, I finished my fifth and last year of school needed to graduate as Perito Mercantil. I immediately left for home. There was another month of classes, from which I was exempted, before the formal graduation. I did not attend my graduation. Later I found out that I had won a prize which included a government job, but, when they realized that I had not been born in Argentina, they gave it to the runner-up. I did not get my diploma because I had not paid the fee. I was not eager to have the diploma. I had no wall to put it on. But my parents thought otherwise and eventually I sent the money and got it, just before we departed for the USA.

I arrived home without any plans of what I would do with my life. Going to university was out of the question under our circumstances. The general outlook for our family was not hopeful. While I was thinking about the big picture, the smaller picture of what I would do next got unexpectedly resolved. The Cooperativa Agricola Ocavi, the colony's cooperative, needed an accountant and offered me the position. It was an easy decision to go for it.

5. THE PENCHANSKY FAMILY

My Aunt Feigl's house, even when they lived in the corrugated iron structure, was a center of social activity. Sonia and I looked forward to Saturday visits to Aunt Feigl's. She had these wonderful children. They were as friendly and good-humored as she was. In the midst of dire deprivation, Saturday at aunt Feigl's was joyous. Sonia and I were part of the gang. The three younger children—Mote, Nechama and Aron, played with us; the older ones looked after us. If I wanted to stay overnight, I slept with Yenie and Riveh who shared a single twin bed. They never showed the slightest hint that I might be imposing on them. That relationship has endured. Continents and oceans have separated us, and sometimes years went by without contact; but when we met, we picked up where we had left off.

The Penchansky family 1947

My older cousins had many friends who also visited on Saturdays. Young men came courting Yenie and Riveh. The children were welcome everywhere. Those poor fellows had to put up with the children if they wanted to see the young women. In that home there was enough warmth to make anyone feel part of the family. Aunt Feigl and my mother managed to bake enough cookies to last the long afternoons. Mate and tea flowed.

Privacy was a luxury that no one dreamed of. The children heard about everything that went on in the household. We followed the romances of my older cousins and voiced our opinions. It was a togetherness that I have never encountered again. Brought about by circumstances, it worked to ameliorate the anguish of isolation.

We lived in a world lacking of beauty, except for the little we could create. The countryside was unattractive, flat and devoid of any natural charm. The land had been cleared of trees, except for a far corner of each farm where some woods were left. In the beginning, small makeshift houses stood scattered in the bare vastness. Almost no trees were left standing to provide shade from the subtropical sun. It was another example of the lack of consideration given to personal comfort in the ICA's grand plan. In time, most farmers had tree groves around their houses.

The priority was physical survival, but cultural hunger gnawed. In the midst of the struggle to produce the necessities to sustain life, in Aunt Feigel's house were hatching all sorts of cultural projects. Some came to fruition. There were people in the colony that had come from Europe with theater experience. They were eager and able to organize a theater group that presented plays.

My first theater experience was a play with Yenie in the lead. I can still evoke the sensation, how overcome I was by the magic of it. I saw Yenie perform in many plays on makeshift stages, with nothing that cost a cent. It was good theater. I loved it especially when it was a comedy. Yenie was a natural comedian. I was fourteen years old when I saw my first film. As fond as I became of films, theater has remained my favorite art form.

Late in 1927, the Penchanskys had arrived in Argentina under the auspices of the Jewish Colonization Association. The ICA settled them on a small plot of land in an older colony, La Capilla, in the province of Entre Rios. They were to stay there until a new colony would be established. They stayed in La Capilla almost two years. They had no money and a father not prone to assume responsibility for his family.

It was up to the children to find a way for the family to survive. The four older children — Yenie, 17, David, 16, Jacobo 14 and Riveh 12, did every kind of labor that they could find to earn food money. They also worked the land they were assigned. Aunt Feigl had never worked at making a living, and besides, she had three younger children—Mote, five, Nechama, three and Aron, an infant. All their efforts did not assure them even enough food for the family, but they stayed together and persevered. They looked forward to better days when they moved to the big farm. They hoped the ICA would help them establish a viable farm.

When we arrived, at the end of May 1931, they had been on the big farm almost two years. They had nothing to show for the whole three and a half years of hard labor, no house, locusts, drought, failed harvests, and the prospect of a decent life less and less likely. They continued the struggle for another couple of years, living in privation and working harder and harder. There was no help from the ICA. By then the ICA was regarded as the enemy.

In 1933, Jacobo was twenty years old. He had worked since childhood. His education was in interrupted episodes, mostly through desperate attempts here and there. Senor Bertozzi had been tutoring him in accounting and whatever else he thought would be useful to the eager young man. Jacobo decided to try his luck in Buenos Aires. There was nothing to lose. He had no decent clothing, but the main problem was that he had no shoes. Footwear in the countryside consisted of *alpargatas* (cloth uppers, rope soles), and if one could afford them, boots for special occasions. All Jacobo owned was a pair of alpargatas. He found someone who owned a pair of shoes his size and was willing to lend them to him. Penniless, with borrowed shoes to mail back, he arrived in Buenos Aires. That marked the beginning of the exodus from the farm to the big city.

Jacobo found work delivering cooking oil by horse and buggy. In Buenos Aires in those days, oil was delivered to homes weekly. The population, being primarily of Spanish and Italian descent, used large quantities of cooking oil. The Spanish had arrived much earlier, but the Italians eventually outnumbered the Spanish. Other than beef, the cuisine was, and still is, predominantly Italian style. Oil is a staple. The more olive oil there is in the mix, the more desirable.

After a while, Jacobo and a fellow deliverer became partners in their own oil delivery business. They bought and mixed oil under their own label. For Jacobo, this beginning led to a steady development of a business career that brought him successes beyond any of his wildest dreams. But not so soon. He had many years of struggle, but was always on the way up. Not long after, Yenie and David arrived. David got a job also delivering oil. I don't know what kind of work Yenie did, but among them they were able to help the family they left behind.

Two years after his arrival in Buenos Aires, Jacobo married Ines Fumberg. This is how he related the circumstances of his marriage decision. The Fumbergs lived in the same complex where Jacobo was living. He had had a few casual conversations with Ines, when her father approached him asking whether he had serious intentions. Before he knew it, he was engaged.

Jacobo was a devoted husband to Ines. He adored and indulged his children. But he never got over the feeling that he had deserted his mother and siblings. He lived torn between peace at home and the compelling desire to help his mother. Ines never understood that. I don't think his mother ever spent a night in their home. Ines came from a different background. Her family was also poor, but each for himself.

Anything Jacobo did for his mother or a sibling was either not known by her or was an occasion for an ugly outburst. There was always some part of his family living in Buenos Aires. Ines found their presence threatening. Later, when Jacobo and Ines were living in great luxury, indulging their children beyond reasonable limits, Ines would tell me about how the relatives were taking advantage of Jacobo. She included among them her own siblings. Jacobo was gregarious and generous. He would have liked a home open to family and friends. That, he never had.

The first year I lived in Buenos Aires to attend school, I often visited them on Sundays. Jacobo was always warm and pleased to see me and Ines tolerated me. I was no threat. They even took me to some grand family weddings of Ines's rich relatives. The country bumpkin was redeemed by being admitted into a good school. I had passed her test.

Years later Jacobo and Ines traveled all over the world. They often came to the United States. The first time they came, Alvin, our three young children and I were living in a Washington suburb. Alvin worked for the Federal Government and I stayed home with the children.

Jacobo liked Alvin, but he immediately concluded that Alvin's occupation held little promise for what he considered a comfortable future. So Jacobo proposed to set us up in a suitable business. Among his enterprises, he had a factory of *dulce de leche*, a caramelized milk product used as jam or syrup. We were to be the United States importers and distributors of *dulce de leche* for his firm. Jacobo presented the plan explaining that the only thing Alvin needed to do was to get a Department of Agriculture license to import the product. He would be responsible for all other arrangements.

The discussion that ensued was a comedy of misperceptions. To start with, there was no way to convince Jacobo that Alvin had no pull to obtain a license from the Department of Agriculture. It was not any easier to explain that Alvin really had other plans for what he wanted to do with his life. Jacobo and Alvin communicated in Yiddish, a language in which Alvin is quite limited. When it got to such serious matters, I became the translator. I went back and forth, not getting anywhere. We ended up amused at the exercise.

Jacobo was one of the most generous people I ever knew. He helped everyone he could. He was moved by social injustice, but his experience taught him that help could only be given on a one-to-one basis. To help anyone, one must have financial means from other sources. In other words, one ought to have a realistic job. He felt that Alvin was naïve to dedicate his life to bringing about social justice. He also thought that I indulged him by supporting him in his pursuit. As I am writing these lines, forty plus years after these events, the Williams Sonoma 2001 Spring Catalog arrived carrying *dulce de leche* from Argentina. It is the first time I have seen it for sale in the United States.

I had made several trips to Argentina before Jacobo died. The last time was in November 1995. Jacobo died January 5, 1997. I always stayed with Jacobo and Ines when I was in Buenos Aires. Jacobo and I had a special affection for each other. The 1995 visit was ominously sad. Jacobo was ill in body and spirit. The tide had turned against him which was a cruel epilogue to a life of caring.

The very people in whom he invested so much let him down. The business that he had built up and eventually given to his eldest son had now gone bankrupt. People with whom Jacobo had done business for many decades lost large amounts of money. Many of them were personal friends. They entrusted their money because they were dealing with Jacobo's son. Jacobo was despondent over the money, the soiling of his name and the havoc it created for his son's family. I do not know the details, but I do know that it was beyond Jacobo's ability to fix. The situation was grim.

For a long time Jacobo had worried about the extravagant lifestyle this son and his family led. There were no limits to their indulgence. Jacobo feared for their future. But he never envisioned the enormity of the debacle that actually happened. Now he was living in physical pain and mental anguish. Jacobo and Ines were cooped up in their apartment, which Ines insisted on keeping dark. Ines sat in the den in front of the television with the remote control in one hand and the bell to summon the maid in the other. I was in the living room and innocently pulled back the drapes and open the door to step out on the balcony. Across the street stood a mansion surrounded by beautiful gardens. It was spring. The sunshine was brilliant. Everything was in bloom. I was basking in the beauty of it when Ines came out to tell me "we don't open the drapes." I never saw the balcony again during the rest of my stay there.

Jacobo had one escape. He kept an office where he went every morning for two or three hours to deal with his real estate investments. Ines described it as a place where people came to ask him for money. She was still worried that he would give away her money.

I had brought a tape recorder to tape conversations with Jacobo. Unfortunately his voice was so weak that very little is clear. I had asked him to tell me about his early life. He wanted to talk about his mother. He explained to me how his mother, my aunt Feigl, had had a hard life from the beginning. She was the eldest of the seven children our grandparents, Alter and Sarah Mishkin, had. She helped to raise the younger ones. Grandmother Sarah had no maid in the early years. Then, when Aunt Feigl married she raised seven children of her own under very difficult circumstances.

She was such a good person. On the farm whenever she baked bread, she saved some for the poor family that lived in a hut on their farm. She died at age sixty-two, just before Jacobo could have given her what she deserved. He was so sorry about that.

It was so unfair. He said to me, "You know, I never said 'no' to my mother." About his early childhood, he had warm memories of spending time with our common grandparents. He remembered Grandfather Alter taking him along on a trip to see the *poritz* (nobleman-landowner). Life in Europe had been better than on the farm. He kept coming back to his mother.

I asked him whether he would like to move away from Buenos Aires. His middle son, Tito, had immigrated to the United States. I thought he might consider living there. He said that what he really wanted was to go to live in Israel. His three sisters now lived there. He loved Israel. He felt at home there. He loved Saturdays at Nechama's, where family and friends gather regularly to enjoy each other's company just as it was in his mother's house. Israel was where he felt most at peace. But that was not a decision for him to make. Ines would not consider it. It was heartbreaking for me to leave him so ill and caught in such an untenable situation.

After Jacobo died his siblings, through the Jewish National Fund, arranged the establishment of a tree grove in his memory. The grove is in a national forest near the Tel Aviv-Jerusalem road, easily accessible for the family to visit. On my recent trip to Israel, Nechama's daughter Nitza drove me to see it. Nitza is an agronomist and has worked for the Jewish National Fund for many years. She picked the place. The memorial plaque is on a large rock that sits on the edge of a hilltop overlooking a lush valley. A spectacular sight. I cannot imagine a more fitting tribute to Jacobo.

David was making his way in Buenos Aires, when he had a most unfortunate accident on his job. A metal shard landed in one of his eyes. In the process of taking out the shard the doctor so damaged the eye that it had to be removed. Besides the physical aspects of the loss of the eye, it was a terrible blow to David's self-confidence. Yenie stayed on in Buenos Aires to care for David until he had recovered enough to go back to work.

David was never the same after the accident. He recovered enough to make progress in business. Then an ill-fated love interest set him back again. He never married. As time passed he became more and more of a loner, spending much of his time by himself listening to his extensive cantorial and classical record collection. He lived in Israel for a few years, moved back to Buenos Aires, and then back again to Israel. He died there, April 20, 1990.

Yenie returned to the farm and eventually married Zev Sklarovsky, who had been waiting for her for years. He was in love with her from the first meeting. She was engaged to marry David Alperin, a distant relative who lived in one of the older colonies. The families knew each other in Europe. David's brother Kalman and his wife Eidle and their five children lived in our colony. Eidle was my mother's and Aunt Feigl's cousin. She expected to be consulted on such a matter. When she heard about it, she set out to break the engagement. She left for her in-laws' home and carried on until she got her way. There was no explanation, not a word from David or anyone else. Silence. Our families shunned Eidle for the rest of the time we lived in Argentina. We continued to have a warm relationship with Kalman and the children.

The story has an ironic ending. Eidle's daughter Ester (to her mother's strong objection) married Mote (Marcos) Penchansky and Eidle spent her last years in their home. And even Yenie took Eidle in and nursed her during an emergency. Zev stayed madly in love with Yenie through their 65-year marriage. He died in April 2000, shortly after their double ninetieth birthday celebration. He had been very ill with cancer for some time. Yenie, the family's tower of strength, was left disconsolate. She was 90 and blind from macular degeneration, and the blow was more than even she could bear. With Zev at her side, she could manage her blindness quite well. He was her eyes, she said.

A year later, when I visited her, we had long conversations not only about the past, but also about current events. She was as clear in mind as ever. I was astonished at her knowledge of what goes on in the country and in the world. She told me that knowing Russian had been her saving grace. Although she had not used the language since she was seventeen, she was able to revive her ability to use it when the influx of Soviet Jews started in Israel. She got much of her information from listening to broadcasts in Russian. With over a million Russian-speaking people in Israel, there are plenty of broadcasts in the language. She did not do nearly as well with Hebrew.

Yenie got audiotapes in Yiddish, Spanish and Russian from the association for the blind. All these acquisitions of languages she made on her long arduous journey came to serve her well in her predicament in old age. It was what kept her from despair. Having first learned Hebrew in her sixties, she complained about how difficult a language it was to learn. While Zev, who had studied it as a youngster, picked it up without difficulty, she never became proficient in it. She died in January 2005 at the age of 95.

Yenie had a good start in life. Being the eldest grandchild she got much attention from her grandparents, aunts and uncles. She was sent away to school with her youngest aunt, my mother. They went to Niezvic, a city with better schools than the *shtetl* of Snov. Yenie finished Russian School in time for the Poles to take over the region where they lived. She then went to Polish school until the family left for Argentina. She also got a Yiddish education. Under the eye of the grandfather, the family somehow was provided for.

My parents described Yenie at 17 to me, as blossoming, smart, self-assured, clever and loved by everyone. When she arrived in Argentina, her life turned upside down. She now was the eldest of seven children in a family without any means to provide for themselves and with an irresponsible father to boot. And there were no grandparents. Her mother was a loving, hardworking and incredibly cheerful person. Her father was totally uninvolved.

This carefree young woman undertook the responsibility to run the family. And she did it with much tenderness and patience through terrible difficulties. More formal schooling for her was out of the question. She learned Spanish here and there, mostly reading whatever was available. She set an example for her siblings. I credit her with making them all into avid readers. My father told me that when he met her again in Argentina, Yenie was a *folkomer mensch* (perfect and complete human being). She was then 21.

A couple of years after they were married, Zev and Yenie settled on an ICA farm far from his and her parents, following the ICA policy not to settle relatives near each other. After a few years of hard work and no progress, they gave up the struggle and moved to Buenos Aires. They started with a grocery store. Later they were in several other businesses. They educated their two daughters, Ester and Judith, in Buenos Aires.

Ester married a Brazilian, Boris Blinder, whom she met on a trip to Israel. They settled in his hometown, Sao Paulo. He was director of a Jewish day school where she was a teacher. They raised three sons. Boris Blinder died in the mid-1990's.

Judith married a young man that swept her off her feet and conned the entire family. The sham lasted long enough for the couple to have a child and for the entire family to be defrauded. The young man managed to flee the country to avoid going to jail. Judith obtained a divorce and with her young child, Dalia, joined her parents who had recently moved to Israel.

Now Zev and Yenie undertook to help Judith reconstruct her life. Though they were still both working full time in their dry-goods store, they lavished full-time loving care on Dalia. They made it possible for Judith to receive the necessary training to have a meaningful professional career. Eventually Judith remarried. Her husband, Lipa Beutel, adopted Dalia. He is the only father Dalia has known. Judith and Lipa have also a son, Moshe.

In my youth, Yenie and Zev often provided me with a warm refuge. In my wanderings they often were in a position and always willing to be helpful. From the age of six, I had a strong attachment to Yenie. When Zev married her, he took the whole package and made it his own. Her devotion to her family became his. Being in their home was a nurturing experience. He cared for everybody she cared for. Zev had a beautiful voice and loved music. He knew cantorial music. He also liked classical music. It was he who exposed me for the first time to opera. Zev got tickets for Yenie, him and me to see a Teatro Colon production in the theater's summer home in the park.

Aron, at the age of eleven, left for Buenos Aires to live with his brother David. He was able to get some schooling while also working with David. Eventually, as soon as it was feasible, Nechama, and for a short time Mote, went to Buenos Aires. Nechama enrolled in the Jewish Teachers' Seminary. She worked during the day and went to school at night for several years until she graduated.

Enia with Nechama Pechansky

At one point, Nechama needed a diploma or equivalency certificate from a government school, which she did not have. Yacov Klainer, a colony exile, who eventually became her husband, was living in Buenos Aires, also working and studying. He found out how this could be accomplished. There was a school district in the City that had a special program for just that. They offered evening classes and a comprehensive test. You could take the test without the classes. Passing the test was all that was needed to get the certificate. The catch was that you had to be a resident of that district. Yacov found someone who lived in that district and was willing to cooperate in a grand scheme by lending his address.

On top of all this, Nechama could not take off from work for the registration. I was recruited to do it—impersonate her. I showed up for the interview with all the information in my purse. When I was asked where I lived, I opened my purse to look for the paper on which the borrowed address was written. Before I produced it, the man looked kindly at me saying, "well, I know now that you don't live in the district, but it's okay; you can register." I filled out the registration form, signed Nechama's name, and so succeeded in my clandestine mission. It was a Woody Allen scene, complete with schlemiel. Nechama took the test, passed and got the certificate.

Mote was the last of the Penchansky children to live full time on the family farm. Aunt Feigl died at the beginning of 1948. Nechama left for Israel not long after. Riveh was married to Shabitay Saul and living on their own farm. The rest were permanently established in Buenos Aires. Mote had his father, Uncle Honye, and Don Francisco to look after. It could not have been an easy life for him. But Mote talks about this time with his usual humor. Mote was and still is a keen humorist. He has an overdeveloped sense of the absurd. His humor is never offensive, but it is sharp.

He also is a master imitator. When we were growing up, there were two individuals who amused people with their unique speech, and Mote could and still can render their speech faultlessly. One was Ivan who was a farm worker at our place for a number of years. He was from some part of Yugoslavia. Ivan wandered all over the world before he landed in Argentina. He spoke seven or eight languages, but not one at a time. He could not separate them. They were merged into one. You needed to know several of them to figure out what he was saying.

The other person was Naumi who was a Saul. The Sauls were Hebrew- speaking Jews from the Middle East. They had never been exposed to Yiddish. They were learning Spanish and Yiddish simultaneously. Naumi spoke her take on Yiddish with great assurance and fluency when she barely knew any. Mote provided us with entertainment.

During this period Mote and Ester Alperin fell in love. They kept it secret from her mother until they decided to get married. Now Eidle, the notorious shrew, had a second chance to play her role. She declared war. Ester was not to see Mote. But Ester is and was, even then at nineteen, a very determined woman. She went on a hunger strike and whatever else it took to prevail. Although she now denies it, I have it on good authority that she was rescued in an emaciated state.

Ester married Mote and undertook to run the household and take care of the two old men. Uncle Honye was often jealous of Don Francisco. Here, juxtaposed, were two men who occupied the opposite extremes of the spectrum of human kindness and a young woman dealing with it. Ester proved equal to the task. One could easily fill a tome and call it fittingly *The Book of Ester*. She became the family guardian angel, caring for everyone that needed care.

All the people who left the farm for the city had a big struggle. The first who left may have struggled a little more than those who followed. But no one that I knew about had it easy. However, the struggle was worth it in every case that I know. At that time, life on the farm was untenable. There was no hope that the future would be better. The ICA was not selling the land and not willing or able to deal with the farmers' plight. Getting out was the only chance at a decent life. Most of those who left did succeed financially to some degree.

Some who made it set themselves up at a distance from recent arrivals which was not unlike the behavior of earlier immigrants towards later comers. There were conspicuous exceptions. When Yenie and Zev arrived in Buenos Aires, they had small quarters, but room for everyone who needed a place to stay. It never changed. I was a beneficiary of their hospitality quite often. Their home was like Aunt Feigl's had been, warm and welcoming. The last year in Argentina, I lived in their house. And the last couple of months, my parents and my two sisters lived there too. It is from their house that we went to the port of Buenos Aires to board a boat that took us to Montevideo where we took the Pan American plane that brought us to New York.

Later when Ester and Mote migrated to Buenos Aires, their home became the central family shelter. Ester took care of everyone who needed help. Those still left in the colony had a place to stay when they needed it. Ester took people to doctors and to the hospital and made arrangements for whatever was needed. She did all that while raising her three children and caring for her aged mother and aged father-in-law. Ester was never affected by any of the city ways. She continued to live by her innate mores.

After years in Buenos Aires and some frightful experiences (holdups and a kidnapping), Mote and Ester moved to Parana where life proved much easier. They have a business and also a farm they purchased from the ICA during the big sell-off. In November 1999, when I visited them, the economic crisis that had been raging for several years had ruined their business, but, at this point in their lives, they were able to weather it. It is not about how much they have as it is about never having aspired to a different lifestyle. Once they could afford what they considered necessities and modest comforts, they were happy to keep their lifestyle and invest in some security for themselves and their children. That proved to be a lucky strategy, because the bottom fell out of the economy and many people were ruined financially.

In March of 2005 when I visited, Ester was running the store and supervising the farm. Mote's health has forced him into almost full retirement. Ester still runs an open house. She keeps in touch with everyone and is always at the ready if someone needs her help. Mote indulges and humors her. What a pair those two make. She is loud and assertive; he is soft-spoken and bullheaded. But they manage to respect each other's ways.

Whenever we meet, the stories about Don Francisco continue. Mote told me about getting Don Francisco to the doctor when he was quite ill. The doctor examined him and took Mote aside. He wanted to know, who was this old man who seemed to mean so much to Mote to bring him there despite his obvious distrust of this kind of medicine. Mote explained to the doctor that Don Francisco was a precious family heirloom entrusted to his care. Then the Doctor explained the seriousness of the illness and gave him medication to administer to the patient. A few weeks later the doctor came to the farm to see Mote's father. He saw Don Francisco busy doing something in the yard and was clearly surprised. Don Francisco smiled at him and said: "Yes, it's me. I know you were sure I would not make it."

6. BARON MAURICE DE HIRSCH

Baron de Hirsch was not a central figure in telling my story when I began. I started to research the origins and development of the colonies as peripheral information. My experience since I left Argentina had led me to conclude that Baron de Hirsch is largely unknown to the Jewish people. I spent eleven years as a demographer for the Jewish Community Federation of Cleveland and during all that time I came across very few people who had ever heard the name Baron de Hirsch. And that was among Jewish-field professionals and lay people active in Jewish affairs. Having grown up with the image of this all-important figure, it seemed strange to me. Could it be that he had been of little importance outside the colonies?

It got stranger and stranger when I started to look for materials. I could get little from Jewish sources directly. As it happened, I was in Paris in March 1999 and visited the grand new Jewish Museum. Since I knew that de Hirsch had lived much of his life in Paris and the main headquarters of the Jewish Colonization Association (official acronym ICA) was there, I was sure I would see much about him in the Museum. That was not the case. I saw no reference to him in any display. When I inquired in the library of the Museum, the librarian could not find a single reference. He had never heard of Baron de Hirsch.

Next, I visited several Jewish bookstores in the Marais, the neighborhood where the Jewish Museum is located. To my request for material on de Hirsch, I got blank stares. One person, as an afterthought, said that the only Hirsch name she ever came across is in "Ecole Lucien de Hirsch," the name of a Jewish school in Paris. She did not know who Lucien de Hirsch was. I soon found out that indeed Lucien was the name of the Baron's son who died at a young age. It was upon his death

92

that the Baron is reported to have said: "My son I have lost, but not my heir; all humanity is my heir." It also appears in another version: "My son I have lost, but not my heir; the Jewish people are my heirs."

Eventually I found assorted material which, through inter-library loans, I was able to examine. Reading the material I found, to my chagrin, that the suffering of the colonists was a planned part of a grand design. Baron de Hirsch had designed a plan to get the Jews away from the Tsar and prevent anti-Semitism by making them into humble farmers. Humiliation was clearly the operating policy. It made me furious. There are references everywhere in the relevant literature to colonists, who lacking necessary skills, abandoned the farms and turned to industry and commerce. That is the excuse the ICA administration used to explain its own failure.

Farming under those circumstances was a heroic undertaking. It was done in Palestine successfully by much the same people. But there people were given a vision and the right to act as free human beings, to make decisions, to find solutions and to change what needed changing. They were not under the yoke of an authoritarian administration, bent on enforcing unreasonable rules in order to implement unworkable plans. In the ICA colonies, people didn't have food or adequate shelter or clothes to keep them warm in cold weather. They worked with the most primitive tools, desperately trying to survive. What necessary skills did they lack?! What arrogance! It is more than arrogance; it is insult and a big lie. In addition to all the physical hardships, they suffered from the despotic and heartless ICA administration, which they distrusted, feared and despised. People who left their farms in those days did it from sheer desperation.

In 1995, I visited my aunt Peshe who still lived on the farm she and her husband, my Uncle Abraham, started in the early 1930's. Her family is among a handful of families who still live on their farms. She was already in her nineties. We talked with sadness about old times and the hardships. Suddenly her eyes lit up and she said, "But all that changed when we got rid of the ICA." Her two sons, Benito and Jacobo, now run a big enterprise. They acquired several other farms and have a viable cattle ranch. And to boot they are educating the children. That is exactly what the ICA tried to prevent. The mission was to grow crops on small farms, have just a few animals and be humble Jews--and especially not to educate the children, because as Baron de Hirsch told Theodore Herzl, "All our misfortunes come from the fact that the Jews want to climb too high. We have too much brains. My intention is to restrain the Jews from pushing ahead. All of the hatred against us stems from this."

In a conversation with my cousin Yenie who at the time was nearing her ninetieth birthday and had been living in Israel for many years, I told her that I was writing about life in the colony. She told me that she often thought about it. She had seen so many immigrants arriving in Israel and how hard it was for them. Then she thought about the ICA colonies and how immigrants were treated there, and she felt the immigrants to Israel were so lucky. Wistfully she added, "Only an ICA agent is capable of taking the last bushel of wheat from a home where there is no bread."

Moritz von Hirsch (later Gallicized to Maurice de Hirsch) was born in Munich, Bavaria in 1831, the son of Joseph and Karoline (Wertheimer) von Hirsch. He was descended from generations of distinguished businessmen and court bankers. His grandfather, Jacob von Hirsch, a banker to the Bavarian royal court, acquired the title of nobility, "von," before his name in 1818, years before Moritz was born. That was not an easy thing for a Jew to attain. It required not only extraordinary achievements, but also considerable measures of flair and aggression.

At 13, Maurice was sent to Brussels to study. At 17, through with school, he went back to Munich and in three years made a sizable fortune in various enterprises. At twenty he joined the firm of Bischoffsheim and Goldschmidt of Brussels, the most important Belgian banking institution with branches in other European capitals.

In 1855, at the age of 24, he married Clara Bischoffsheim. She was the daughter of the senior partner of the firm, Senator Bischoffsheim. By all accounts, she was an extraordinary person, smart, highly educated and generous of spirit. She spoke French, German, English and Italian. In her early twenties, she was already involved in charitable causes, Jewish as well as in the greater community. She was a natural philanthropist, following the family tradition.

Soon after his marriage, de Hirsch left Bischoffsheim and Goldschmidt to establish his own firm. From the start, he was interested in railway construction. When an opportunity presented itself, he was ready. Through a complex set of circumstances, he obtained the concession from the Ottoman government to build railways in the Ottoman Empire with links to the European system. He established the Oriental Railway Project to carry out the mission of building what came to be known as the Orient Express which linked London and Constantinople.

While the concept itself was masterful, the undertaking of dealing with the numerous governments, where encounters with anti-Semitism were sure to occur, was the ultimate in self-confidence. The Baron was richly endowed with ability, courage, and chutzpah. He worked out the financing, the construction and, for lack of alternatives, at times, even the running of a railway, all the while with anti-Semitism lurking around him. The Oriental Railway was his masterpiece. It earned him a prominent place in 19th century economic and industrial history. Today, those who study 19th century economics are probably the group that is most likely to know his name and accomplishments.

Baron Maurice de Hirsch made a great fortune. He owned estates and businesses in a number of countries and he consorted with royalty. He worked at acquiring acceptance among the nobility as his ancestors had done before him. He was even more skillful at it than they had been. He did not take rejection with tolerance. Legend has it that a Paris club that refused him membership ended up as a stable for the Baron's horses. In 1890 his fortune was estimated to be equivalent to several billion dollars today.

Many considered Baron Maurice de Hirsch the greatest Jewish philanthropist of the 19th century. In the last ten years of his life, he gave away unprecedented sums to charitable causes. The ICA was the recipient of the largest share. He promptly answered calls for help through the Alliance Israelite Universelle in all corners of the Jewish world. The Baroness Clara, his wife, was the moving force behind this philanthropy. She continued it after the Baron's sudden death in 1896, until her death in 1899. "The 14th edition of the Encyclopaedia Britannica, published in 1929, still referred to JCA [alternate for ICA] as probably the greatest charitable trust in the world."

The Baron and Baroness had a son and a daughter. The daughter died in infancy. The son, Lucien, died in 1887 at the age of thirty-one, from pneumonia. He was unmarried, but left a "natural child," a daughter. The Baron also had two "natural children," who survived him. I found the following reference: "Even if he was not faithful as a husband, he was singularly happy in his marriage, and his wife Clara showed sufficient largeness of heart to refer in her will to his two illegitimate children as her 'adopted children' and to make provision for them on top of what he had given them in his lifetime."

Baron de Hirsch died of a heart attack while on a hunting trip at his country estate in Ogyalle, Hungary in April of 1896, at the age of 64. As the obituaries in the Viennese press noted, Hirsch lately had always been seen accompanied by two young boys whose mother had been English ['Neues Wiener Abendblatt,' April 21, 1896] or American ['Neue Freie Presse,' April 22, 1896]. Their name was given as Forreste-Bischoffsheim. The younger of the two, Raymond (1880-1912) died young.

The older [Arnold] (b. 1879) then known as Count of Bendern, lived in Vaduz, Liechtenstein. The "Semi Gotha" of 1912 [p. 146] claims that on his mother's side Arnold, holder of a twenty year old barony which in 1900 was confirmed for Great Britain by Royal Decree, hailed from old French aristocracy, de Forrestier. And we learn from the 1956 "Who's Who" of his education at Eton and Oxford, his army and war service, and his membership in Parliament. In 1932 he became a natural citizen of the Principality of Liechtenstein, which made him a hereditary count and Diplomatic Counsellor. A London Society weekly, after referring to the sporting achievements of this good-looking and wealthy Liberal M.P. tells us that he was rejected by the Reform Club ['The Bystander' February 12, 1913]. This was allegedly because of the role he played in the agitation for land reform, which the wealthy and respectable Whig landowners abhorred. And Lloyd George and Winston Churchill, who had sponsored his membership, resigned from the Club."

Baron de Hirsch was an avid collector of civic honors. He received decorations from Turkey, Austria, Italy, France, Belgium and probably additional countries. He was not above using devious methods, when necessary, to obtain one, especially if he perceived that anti-Semitism was an obstacle. "Hirsch was anxious to obtain nobility for his offspring. We are told that his son Lucien (died October 20, 1888) was the first Jew to obtain a Belgian barony. Hirsch also tried hard and apparently successfully) to obtain nobility for his natural sons, Arnold and Raymond de Forest, but was less successful in the case of Lucien's natural daughter Lucienne, who later married the banker E. Balser." (From "Turkenhirsch" by Kurt Grunwald, page 106).

Baron de Hirsch in his earlier years answered calls for help by Jewish and non-Jewish charities. His wife, the Baroness Clara, was keenly aware of the desperate situation of the Jews in Russia (Russia at the time encompassed much of what we call now Eastern Europe) and elsewhere. Her father and other members of her family had long been leaders in the Alliance Israelite Universelle, a Jewish charitable organization founded in the mid-nineteenth century to help Jews in need anywhere.

The Baroness is credited with exposing her husband to the plight of oppressed Jews and encouraged him to put his energy into helping them. He was from the start a firm believer that the only worthwhile charity is "economic rehabilitation." He experimented in several rural areas with providing training for Jews to become artisans and farmers.

When the Baron retired in the 1880's, he dedicated himself almost exclusively to his philanthropic interests. He looked for a solution to the problem of the disenfranchised and persecuted Jews of Russia. Pursuing his original plan he wanted to create schools across Russia to train the Jews from the *shtetls* as artisans and farmers. He offered the Russian government fifty million francs for the implementation of the plan. The Russian government was willing to take the money without commitment to the plan. Baron de Hirsch gave up dealing with the Tsar's government and looked elsewhere for a solution to the problem of the Russian Jews.

Baron de Hirsch designed a grand plan. It was based on the romantic notion that working the land is ennobling and his conviction that anti-Semitism would disappear if Jews became rooted in the soil. He was determined to return them to working the soil. This would make them useful members of society: a normal people.

He looked for a country with vast uncultivated expanses of arable land and a friendly government. Starting in the early 1880's, he sent experts to a number of countries to explore the possibilities of establishing farm colonies. One of the countries was Palestine, which did not meet any of the Baron's requirements. Brazil, Canada, and some others passed, but Argentina fit the bill to a tee. And the price was right.

He envisioned moving hundreds of thousands, or even millions, of Russian Jews to Argentina over several decades. The plan included the repayment by the colonists of all expenses. That money would be used to bring the next group. He founded the Jewish Colonization Association (ICA) to implement and administer his plan. The ICA was incorporated in London in

1891. There was some advantage to doing this under English law. The main headquarters remained in Paris.

The Argentine government offered the ICA philanthropic status and, soon after, ICA agents proceeded to purchase land in several Argentine provinces. Eventually about one and a half million acres were acquired. The largest part was in the province of Entre Rios. Desperate Jews fleeing from persecution in Eastern Europe ended up in Argentina even before the colonies were ready.

In 1891, a group of 900 Russian Jews, on their way to Palestine, were stranded in Constantinople, the seat of the Ottoman Empire. Palestine was under Ottoman rule. The Russian Jews needed the Ottoman authority's permission to enter Palestine, but they were refused. When they were stranded without money, someone contacted Baron de Hirsch on their behalf. He immediately responded and arranged for their transportation to France from where he sent them on to Argentina. After all the misadventures they endured, they arrived to where a colony had been planned. There was nothing there. They rioted to get food and materials to build shelters. That is how the colony named Maurice in the province of Buenos Aires started.

There were a number of tragic incidents with fleeing Russian Jews. In 1889, before the ICA acquired any land, a group of 800 Russian Jews from a place called Podolia disembarked in Buenos Aires ready to claim the land to which they believed they had title deeds. An Argentine government agency in Paris, charged with promoting immigration, was the culprit in this misdeed. The stranded people went through unspeakable horrors. Many of the young children died during the time they wandered and waited. Eventually they became the first settlers of the colony of Moises Ville in the province of Santa Fe.

In the early stages of the colonization, there were many such stories. Rioting became a problem to the ICA and the answer was to send disciplinarians to make the colonists behave. The riots occurred out of desperation when survival was at stake, when there was nothing to lose.

We arrived in 1931, forty years later. People had not been streaming in on their own accord for a long time. ICA agents were travelling through the Eastern European *shtetls,* asking Jews to go. But the conditions on arrival were not much improved. It was treacherous, especially for those who came without any money. We heard and witnessed much suffering aggravated by the callousness of the ICA agents.

I have pondered what might have happened had Baron de Hirsch lived longer. Would he eventually have recognized the shortcomings of his plan and modified the ICA policies? Being a businessman, he could not have failed to recognize failure when he saw it, I reasoned. But for the six years that he was running the operation, no catastrophe was big enough for him to consider any changes. In the first six years he had six administrators in Buenos Aires. He insisted on enforcement of his commandments. His commandments were that the colonists must work 15- hour days seven days a week; have no hired labor, even for jobs for which they lacked the required implements; show no sign of aspiring to have more than subsistence; and expel all those who did not live up to these conditions. There were no commandments to treat the colonists with consideration or kindness or to try to ameliorate their suffering.

An early administrator worthy of special mention was Albert E. W. Goldsmid, once a colonel in the British Army. Goldsmid was what we call today a Jew by choice. His father was born a Jew, but converted to Christianity and made a career in the British Indian Civil Service. While making his career in the British Army, Albert E. W. Goldsmid got interested in his roots and proceeded to undo his father's deed by converting to Judaism. He was interested in helping fellow Jews who were in trouble. He had also given some thought to the problems of the Jewish people and was active in Chovevei Zion, an early Zionist movement. Goldsmid was well connected to British nobility, which impressed the Baron. Both the Baron and Goldsmid wanted to help the oppressed Jews of Eastern Europe to escape their oppressors, but differed in the ultimate aims. Goldsmid saw the Argentine colonies as a way station and preparation for the Jewish State, a reenactment of Moses' plan, while the Baron saw it as a goal in itself.

The Baron saw in the Colonel a trained tough administrator, one who could enforce discipline. He sent him off to Buenos Aires with strict instructions to take hold and straighten out the ungrateful colonists. The first thing Goldsmid did was to tour the colonies. He found out that the disturbances were caused by unjust treatment. He corrected some injustices, instituted some reforms, expelled a few who obviously could not do the work necessary to survive, and even arranged for the ICA to pay passage for some who wanted to leave the country.

Goldsmid lasted just little over a year. He could not deal with the Baron's interference. The next administrator was the first from Eastern Europe. The hope was that having a language in common with the colonists would help. But this one did not succeed either. Arrogance of power was built into the job and those wretched colonists knew enough to hate it. So it went, as far as I can tell, with every successive administrator.

The extent of Baron de Hirsch's conviction that his financial philanthropy gave him the right to wield unlimited power over people is chilling. Lucien Wolf, a journalist, in an interview with the Baron reported:

> "We chatted for over an hour about his Argentine Scheme and Jewish matters generally, he talking throughout in that inimitable Jewish vein, which is a compound of shrewdness and quiet humor, of irony and pathos with here and there a flash of genuine racial pride. That his heart was in his great scheme and that it was a thoroughly Jewish heart, I am convinced. I shall not soon forget the tenderness with which he said, as he looked at one of my photographs: 'Dear me! How interesting it is to see these old Jewish faces under the Argentina sun. See this sad-faced man carrying his

bundle of sticks, still clad in his Polish old coat; and these little Hebrew cowboys who have passed from the Ghetto to the open country of the New World... When my Scheme is a success it will bring shame to the cheek of every Russian. The time will come when I shall have three or four hundred thousand Jews flourishing on their homesteads in the Argentine, peaceful and respectful...'

He then told me about a family he sent out, of which the father has been a professor, and the daughters were well educated girls, accomplished musicians and linguists, and who were then all following the plough at Entre Rios. 'Yes,' he added, 'they give me the greatest hope.'" ["Turkenhirsch" by Kurt Grunwald p.121-122 from "Glimpses of Baron de Hirsch," "Jewish Chronicle," May 8, 1896].

Goldsmid's idea turned out to be prophetic. The Jews who went to the colonies were saved from the Holocaust and a large number of them or their children or grandchildren ended up in Israel. They did not need the colony experience to become "a normal people," but they needed a place to go to survive. Something good came of the Baron's efforts, after all.

My husband, Alvin, and I, and our children Jessica, Ken and Wendy went on our first trip to Israel in 1962. We stayed with my cousins Nechama and Yacov Klainer and their four children Tsipora, Nitza, Hanan and 3-month old Giora. They were living in Kfar Argentina, an agricultural community made up of Jews from the Argentine colonies. The Klainers had a small house, but somehow they managed to put us all up. The children lacked a common language, because ours knew only English then. Theirs knew Hebrew, Spanish and Yiddish. But not having a common language did not stop them from playing together, teaching each other games and songs. They became friends for life.

The name Kfar Argentina is gone. It was changed to Nir Zvi. It is no longer an agricultural community. It has become a dormitory suburb of Tel Aviv. The Klainers have a compound now on their piece of land. Each of their two sons has built a house and lives there with his family. Nechama's home is the gathering place for family and friends every Saturday, reminiscent of her mother's house many years ago. The Klainer children all speak good English and ours have acquired additional languages, but the new generation is not yet there. Jessica and Allen, her husband, and their children, Talia and Jeremy, have recently returned from a visit to Israel. They stayed part of the time at the Klainer compound, and Talia and Jeremy repeated their mother's experience from thirty-seven years ago.

Whenever I am in Israel, I hear about the great contribution the Argentine Jews have made in Israel. I see more of my childhood friends in Israel than on my visits to Argentina. What a long hard way they have traveled! Israel did not need them all to be farmers. Israel needed exactly what they were, some of everything, and not illiterate. Had the ICA cared about the people it lorded over, it could have saved many more Jews from the Holocaust. The flow stopped once the colonies fell into disrepute. Instead the resources and energy were spent on a large bureaucracy hell-bent on implementing an absurd social engineering experiment.

In comparing the legacies of Baron de Hirsch and Theodore Herzl, I find all the ingredients of a classic folk tale: Man playing God versus listening to the people, the power of money versus the power of an idea, blaming the victim instead of the circumstances. These two men who met in 1895, passionately wanted to solve the problem of their people. Had they been able to work together, the chances of a solution would have been enhanced beyond imagination. But they saw the problem, and therefore the solution, in entirely different lights. There was no meeting of the minds.

Herzl was hoping for another chance to persuade Baron de Hirsch of the soundness of his convictions, but the Baron died suddenly in 1896, before such a meeting was arranged. Herzl died in 1904. In both cases the work of implementing their ideas were left to other people. Baron de Hirsch left a richly endowed, legally established organization, with explicit rules and regulations. Never doubting that he had all the answers, he left no room for alternatives, exceptions or adjustments. Herzl left a vision that he had presented to the Jewish people for discussion. Between 1897 and 1903 he convened six world Jewish congresses. Whatever the arguments and dissensions, and there were many, the masses were with him on the core of his vision, a Jewish homeland in Palestine. For money, his followers used the ubiquitous blue and white *pushke* (small box) to collect coins from the common people. We know the outcome--just like good fable would have it.

The number of biographies is used as a measure of the historical importance of a person. To date, more than a century after his death, there has not been a comprehensive biography of Baron Maurice de Hirsch.

7. THE ABRAHAM GUIRCHOVICH FAMILY

Uncle Abraham was 26 years old and single when he came with us to Argentina. He had left his parents' home where he worked with his father in the cheese making business.

Abraham lived with us and worked with my father through the harsh period of settling down and creating a functioning farm in such an inhospitable place. Neither brother had ever done anything that would have prepared them for such work. To earn some spending money, Abraham joined Jacobo Penchansky in the enterprise of cutting down trees for lumber, grueling work given the primitive tools at their disposal. But the young men were desperate.

The memory of my uncle in that period is all about food. I only saw him at mealtime. He was out at work most of the time. He spent the little free time he had with the young people. Uncle Abraham enjoyed food, any food my mother prepared. Whenever she could take the time she would prepare his favorite dish, blintzes. Once when the Penchansky boys were visiting, Mother made a large quantity of blintzes for a contest of who could eat the largest number. Uncle Abraham was the winner.

Sometime in the second year, Uncle Abraham met and married Peshe Alperin, the daughter of settlers in one of the older colonies. Her family came from the same area in Europe and may have been distantly related. Peshe's brother Kalman Alperin and his family lived on a farm in our colony in an area called El Sauce. That is where they met. When Uncle Abraham announced his plans to leave and get married, my father was devastated and angry. Mother was angry at my father for being angry. She told him it was unfair for him to have taken his brother for granted. Father didn't talk to his brother. He soon got over it. Peshe was a suitable wife for Abraham and easy to like. My parents gave the newlyweds some animals as a wedding gift and life went on.

The ICA strictly enforced rules of separating families and placed Abraham and Peshe as far as possible from us on the other side of Alcaraz, in an area called Paiticu. It was impossible for us to visit my uncle's family or for them to visit us because one would have to stay overnight to do so. No farmer could leave his farm for even one night, and if it rained, he might not be able to return the next day. I do not remember ever visiting my aunt and uncle at their home, or any holiday or other celebration that brought the two families together. Fortunately, the ICA could not keep track of the family relationships of women in the colony, so my aunt Peshe became a neighbor to her sister Dishe Bresler. The two sisters were helpful to each other, and their children grew up as close cousins. The brothers saw each other in Alcaraz by chance or by sending word to arrange an encounter.

Uncle Abraham's farm was much closer to Alcaraz than ours. Children from that area attended the school there. At age ten, when I began school and lived in Alcaraz, Uncle Abraham came to pick me up one Saturday after school. He bought me an ice cream cup before we set out for his farm. Ice cream was an exotic treat. Ice had to be brought from a long distance. As soon as it arrived, one of the merchants would make ice cream by hand without any special implements. It had to be consumed before the ice melted.

We set out for Uncle Abraham's home, with me happily holding the ice cream cup. I licked the ice cream gingerly, planning to leave some for Benito, my one-year-old cousin that I was about to meet. Uncle Abraham kept on urging me to finish it before it melted, but I kept a half cup of melted ice cream firmly in my hand. We arrived at the farm, and Aunt Peshe came out to greet us with Benito in her arms. Benito was a big, blond, healthy-looking whopper of a boy. I offered him the cup of melted ice cream; he gave it a whack and it splashed all over me.

It did not take long for Benito to warm up to me and enjoy my attention. I stayed until Sunday afternoon when Uncle Abraham brought me back to Alcaraz. I was well aware what a sacrifice it was for them to give all that precious time to bring me to their home. I visited them again a number of times, sometimes getting a ride with a neighbor. There were several children nearby for me to play with, including Peshe's nieces and nephews, the Bresler children.

Their house was in a cluster of four houses sharing one water pump powered by a windmill. The windmill was there when the ICA bought the land. Windmills were off the ICA's list of necessities. A windmill was a significant improvement over a primitive pump. But four farmers sharing one source of water caused frictions during droughts when farmers were in fear of losing their animals. During such stressful times, water became the tinder that sparked bitter disagreements.

Uncle Abraham and Aunt Peshe fit the ICA ideal faultlessly. They loved the land, were hardworking, had modest expectations and, to make it perfect, had two sons, Benito and Jacobo who took to farming with great zeal. Their daughter, Rosita, escaped to Buenos Aires as soon as she got a chance. The family lived through the hardest of times without ever thinking of giving up. With the exception of Rosita they were wedded to the land for better or for worse. But they despised the ICA, their oppressor. The hard work, the droughts, the locust and the other plagues they could handle, if only the ICA would sell them the land and disappear. Their dream was to get rid of the ICA.

When they finally bought the land in November 1947, life became complete. Benito set out to buy as many of the abandoned farms as he could. He described to me his father's fear at incurring so much debt and his insistence that they needed the land to make the farm viable. It was their chance for a more secure existence, he pleaded. Abraham signed the papers with much apprehension. Benito and Jacobo went on to build a sizable enterprise working harder and harder. Abraham soon realized how right Benito had been when he urged him to acquire more land. He put his full confidence in his sons, and they made him very proud.

By the time the ICA began selling the land to the farmers, many of them had abandoned the land. The hopelessness had been driving them away for years. Much of the land was vacant. Few of those who purchased the land from the ICA remained on the farms. Older people retired to the village of Alcaraz, from where they could oversee the hired workers on their farms. Others went to Parana or other cities and became absentee landlords. But not the Guirchovich family. They stayed and did the hard work, albeit with better equipment, and continued the old-fashioned farmer's way of life. The sons worked along the hired help in the fields and forests, while the parents ran the household and cared for the animals and plantings near the house. Benito and Jacobo were among a handful of Jewish young men left in the colony. The Jewish young women were long gone.

Uncle Abraham and Aunt Peshe had a loving relationship. They supported each other in every way. Peshe, unlike my mother, did not complain, nor did she tell her children that this was not a life for them, that there was a world out there where they belonged, that they had to get some education. They had a peaceful and loving home, even when there was no food. They had a long struggle. It began to diminish as the children got older. They worked from an early age, while still in school. By then Alcaraz offered a full primary school education and was reachable from home. That is as much schooling as they got. Rosita wanted to continue her education, but it was too embarrassing even to ask for such a luxury under the family's circumstances. It wasn't until the youngest, Jacobo, finished primary school that the subject of further education came up, but was not pursued, because he was not interested.

Aunt Peshe was remarkably resilient. In the early years, she worked alongside her husband doing hard physical work. She did the milking of the cows at dawn. Somehow she managed to find the energy to help whenever a crisis struck somebody in the family. She raised her own three children and, when her cousin Shloime Stirin's wife fell mentally ill, he brought his two-month-old Shifre to Peshe to raise. She raised her until she was age six and ready for school. Helping came naturally to her. She did not look strong, nor was she without health problems, but she lived to the age of ninety-six. In her seventies and eighties she was a live-in grandmother helping raise three grandchildren. Abraham was strong and healthy and died at seventy-two of pancreatic cancer.

Benito, the eldest, never married. In 1981, Jacobo at forty married Mabel, a 26-year-old Catholic young woman from a neighboring area. There was an agreement that the children were to be raised Jewish. Abraham had died already. Peshe gave her blessings. Now the household consisted of four adults. In the next five years three children were added, Abraham, Malka and Libia. Mabel proved to be a match for the Guirchovich family. She has worked as hard and is just as committed to their way of life. She demanded nothing more than what was already there. She is an extraordinary homemaker, cook, baker, seamstress, knitter, quilt maker and more. Besides housework, she tends to a large vegetable garden and assorted small animals. She explains that she helps the men with things that require more agility or dexterity than they have. I do not think she ever asked or even wanted a real house. They keep repairing and expanding the barrack-like 70-plus-year-old original structure and filling it with appliances. Aunt Peshe never aspired to have a real house either.

In her old age, Peshe used to spend time at Rosita's home in Buenos Aires. Rosita would come to get her and also bring her back. It was a six-hour overnight ride by bus. Nearing the mid-nineties, Peshe fell ill, and her last couple of years were very difficult. Old age had caught up with her. Her mind remained clear, but her body was coming apart. She suffered a slow death and the family suffered with her. She prayed to God to let her die. She was nursed at home to the end.

A development that gave me great pleasure was hearing that all three children were sent away to school. Somehow that became a must, not a luxury. Mabel, I think, was the main force behind that decision. She talked to me about it with such passion, pride and determination, no Jewish mother could overmatch.

Whatever it would take, her children were going to get an education. Abraham, Malka and Libia attended the Jewish Teachers' Seminary in Moises Ville in the bordering province of Santa Fe. They were among the last students of the school. The Seminary was created in 1943 and for more than a half century supplied teachers for Jewish schools all over Argentina. The Seminary provided room and board, and it functioned in conjunction with the government secondary school. In the Seminary the children blossomed. They were exposed to a cultural ambiance and ate it up. They acted in plays, went on trips and participated in all sorts of social and cultural activities.

Besides getting a substantial Jewish education, Abraham and Malka finished the regular secondary school. The youngest, Libia, finished her secondary education in a special school, one that emphasizes agrarian subjects. Since early childhood she has been an animal lover. She knew she wanted to be a veterinarian the day she learned there was such a profession.

As I am writing this chapter, Abraham is nearing the end of a six-year course in agronomy, Malka is pursuing a five-year course in rural administration and Libia is in veterinary school. These children are as wedded to the land as their grandparents were. The tradition is solidly being carried into the future.

Rosita, from early childhood, helped her mother with the work and grew up to be a nurturer like her. As a young woman Rosita went to Israel for a year, where she learned to speak Hebrew. She returned as she had promised her parents, but she was not willing to stay on the farm. She went to Buenos Aires and worked in a jewelry store for a few years. She married Iser Erlich, an accountant who loves to garden. That is as close as she wants to be to agriculture. They raised and educated two sons, Leonardo and Ruben.

Rosita runs her home with warmth and pleasure. She enjoys cooking, baking, and receiving guests. Iser is a loving husband who encourages her to do anything she enjoys. In her late sixties, she still attended cooking classes. For years, she has been a member of an Israeli dancing group of seniors. Unlike her parents and brothers, she is curious about the larger world. She knows the city of Buenos Aires thoroughly. Her way of life is alien to her family and it pains her that the only way she sees them is when she goes to visit them. They never come to visit her. They do not travel. Television seems to be the only form of entertainment they have. Lately, they acquired a cell phone, which makes it possible for family to reach them. They are loving and hospitable people, but live in isolation.

When I left Argentina, Benito, Rosita and Jacobo were 12, 9 and 5 and I hardly knew them. It was during my trips back that I got to know them. My first trip back was with Alvin, my husband, in November 1966. I hadn't seen the Guirchovich family in 20 years. Uncle Abraham, Aunt Peshe and cousins Benito and Jacobo gave us an overwhelmingly warm reception. Rosita was living in Buenos Aires already. Times were much better. Uncle Abraham exuded pride in his boys' accomplishments.

Indeed changes had taken place. The ICA was long out of the picture. They now owned the land and, having bought a number of additional farms, the larger acreage made it into a vital enterprise. They radically changed the operation by abandoning the pursuit of the dream of a good harvest that seldom materialized. It was now a cattle ranch. As they had thrown off the ICA yoke, not only did the economic situation change, but the psychological did even more. They worked as hard as before and have continued to this day. And to this day, they have not built a real house nor taken a vacation. Their only outings seem to be visits to doctors. I once asked Rosita how her mother's life changed when the ICA left. She thought for a while and said: "For one thing, she no longer milks cows in mud up to her knees." They were prosperous and they were happy. They had a generator and appliances, shiny machinery and outbuildings. They also had a new Peugeot and, miraculously, a paved road to drive it on.

An auspicious development was the building of a paved road which goes through their farm by their house. It is the one and only paved road for many miles around and part of the Pan American Highway. It presents some very amusing situations for them. They often get unexpected visitors as a consequence of being the only house in the vicinity reachable by car when a rain turns the unpaved roads impassable. People caught by rain on the paved road can always make it to the Guirchovich house for shelter.

While we were there, Benito and Jacobo left to take cattle to the market and did not come back that evening. The next morning, I noticed that they hadn't slept in their beds. I wondered why Peshe was not worried. When I asked her about it, she said: "Oh, that is because you cannot go to sleep with cash in hand; you may wake up having lost most of it." The inflation was so high and unpredictable that money could lose much of its value overnight. The sons don't go to sleep until they have invested it. They were out looking for a deal.

Argentina has had terrible economic crises, some caused by what we call "acts-of-God "and others by bad government. The Guirchovich family has had hard times, but they have weathered crisis after crisis with courage and determination not to lose any of the land.

8. WORK AND PARTING

Back in Alcaraz, I lived in Mrs. Perlstein's home where my sister Sonia had lived when she was attending school there. Mrs. Perlstein was a remarkable woman. She owned what we then called a boliche, a small store where the native population came to have a drink and some food and to buy assorted other items. Boliches in that region have now evolved into trendy places where young people come to dance. But in those days they were cheap saloons. Mrs. Perlstein was attractive in looks and demeanor. She carried herself with great dignity in all circumstances. She could handle a drunk without raising her voice. Her husband, who came from a respectable, prosperous family, turned out to be a scoundrel. She tried hard to reform him, but, once she realized that it was not possible, she physically threw him out of the house. He had squandered all their money. With few options, she opened a boliche and was able to raise and educate her two daughters on her own. The daughters ended up in Buenos Aires.

I found work at the Cooperative interesting. I learned to apply what I had learned at school while dealing with people and issues I cared about. The general manager (gerente), Isaac Greis, was an able administrator and easy to work with. He was generous with help in getting me started. The Cooperative was both a producers' and consumers' cooperative patterned after the British Rochedale model. It carried out a wide variety of functions. It bought all the products the farmers produced and sold them on the market. It also ran a general store with a full range of merchandise in demand by the farmers. It was a member of the Fraternidad Agraria, the central organization of all the cooperatives in the ICA colonies. The Fraternidad Agraria was the only organization that took on the ICA about the injustices it perpetrated on the farmers, albeit seldom successfully. The Fraternidad Agraria was a thorn in the ICA's side. It needled them, but the ICA had the arrogance of an imperial ruler that would not be moved.

At its peak in 1940, the colony had nearly two hundred farmers. By the end of 1943, there were at least thirty abandoned farms. Nearly all of the farmers were members of the Cooperative. I interacted with most of them and got to know many of them. They were a motley lot and, considering their hard life, they possessed a remarkable sense of humor. I came to believe that their humor was heightened by the hopelessness of their situation.

At that time, the exodus of the young was not yet complete. There were still a few young people around, mostly young men. The young women were the first to leave. Farming depended heavily on sons, and, for a son to leave, especially the only or last one, meant putting the parents in jeopardy. My life at that time was as if in suspension. I did not have a next step. All I knew was that I was not going to stay there long. It was for the moment a time to relax and try not to worry about the future.

The War was still raging in Europe, and the worry of what happened to the family members who were left there was the major concern. The war in the Pacific was not ours, although we knew how important it was to win it. The possibility of going to the U.S was not discussed. I saw family and friends and went to dances and other social gatherings.

Most of the other young people were also at loose ends. Although some of them seemed to like farming, none wanted to be ICA farmers. And there was no sign that the ICA would ever relent and sell the land to them. The ICA did suddenly wake up to the fact that their colonies were dying. Their ignorance of the magnitude of their failure was manifested in the remedy they produced. They sent traveling cultural emissaries to arrange social activities for young people. That was a pail of water to save a burning house.

Sonia was in school in Concordia. She was living in the home of a Hebrew teacher. I went to visit her one weekend and took my

3-year-old sister Ines along. I took some farm products, cheese, sausages and some other foods. The family seemed friendly and Sonia seemed comfortable there. But at meal time, I realized that these people were scrimping on food. They were starving my sister. Even the food I brought was portioned out in minute quantities. I was appalled. When I asked Sonia about it, her answer was that that was how this family ate. Sonia, who had been the slender member of the family, did not need this experience. I did not know what to do about it, except to make sure Sonia always had money to buy additional food. We agreed not to tell our parents and never did.

Life continued without change or hope until the jolt delivered by the end of the War in Europe. Soon after the good news of our side winning, the horrendous news started arriving. Our world stood still in shock. Everyone was directly affected. A general numbness permeated as the details kept coming in. Sometime after, that my father finally broke down and admitted that he was ready to give up the struggle. He could not bear the thought of having to send Ines away to school. Ines was not yet five at the time.

That set in motion the plan of renewing our place on the waiting list of applicants for immigration to the U.S. It had been about twenty years since my parents got on that list. Mother wrote to one of her siblings, probably Sam or Leike, asking them to do the required sponsorship papers. They recruited a sponsor of substantial means to guarantee that we would not become a burden on the U.S. government. None of mother's four siblings qualified, I surmise. In the latter part of 1945, we were notified that we could expect to be called within a year. The plan was for me to go immediately to Buenos Aires to be near the American Embassy in order to expedite the process.

I resigned my job at the Cooperative, giving them several weeks' notice to find my replacement. They hired a local young woman, Dinke Lev, our neighbor, who was halfway through the commercial school course. She was not ready, but I am sure she could have been easily trained to do the work. She was bright and eager to learn. But I was too preoccupied with myself to think of helping her. She was let go. If I had stayed an extra month, she would have been able to keep the job. It was a thoughtless thing I did. I have regretted it all these years.

I left for Buenos Aires where I lived with my cousins Yenie and Zev Sklarovsky. I found a job in the office of an architect-developer, Jacobo Erlijman. It was centrally located within walking distance of the American Embassy. I saw a lot of the Embassy during that year. I was anxious to get the visas and be able to send the good news to my parents. I remember the innumerable times I heard "not yet" and finally, "they have arrived." My next responsibility was to get us boat passages. Flying was beyond what we could afford. I set out to canvass every ship company in Buenos Aires and talk to anybody who could possibly help me find passages, be it on a passenger or cargo ship. For what seemed endless weeks and weeks, I was running all over Buenos Aires following leads and promises that ended unsuccessfully.

While I was going through all these preparations for emigration, I began to think about what this meant for me personally. I thought about being an immigrant, speaking with an accent for the rest of my life. I was familiar with the prejudices immigrants usually encounter. I was not a citizen of Argentina. Getting citizenship was an expensive process that required hiring a lawyer. I had not given it any thought yet. One could not vote until age twenty-two, anyway. My parents never considered becoming citizens of Argentina, and neither did the other immigrants in the colony. It was not in the ICA's design. The original agreement between the ICA and the Argentine government was that the colonists could only remain in the country as long as they remained on the farms. The ICA agreed to remove anyone that left or was expelled from one of their colonies from the country.

This was done until it became impossible for the ICA to handle. I had wanted my parents to leave the farm and move to a city. My father could not bear to abandon his "investment," and my mother was waiting to go to the United States. My attachment to the country was not insignificant. However, getting my parents freed from the ICA's bondage did override all other considerations.

Meanwhile, my parents proceeded to liquidate the farm. They sold the livestock, the equipment and their personal possessions. The house, outbuildings, fences and other improvements were abandoned. I was not there to see them go through it. I do not know whether there was a settlement with the ICA -- by this I mean whether the ICA extracted any payment from my parents, because, according to the ICA, every farmer was always deeply in debt to them. I know there were good-bye gatherings. I can imagine the sadness of the scene where my mother said good-bye to her sister Feigl, whom she never saw again. Feigl died just over a year later. And the parting of my father and his brother Abraham must have been equally wrenching. They were the only surviving members of their original family, having lost everyone else in the Holocaust. Mote told me that the saddest sight of all was the embrace between my father and Don Francisco.

While doing the research for this memoir, I was shocked to find out that it was just one year after my parents abandoned the farm that the ICA, forced by the government, began to sell the land to the farmers at advantageous prices and conditions. My parents' 15-year experience in Argentina was fraught from beginning to end with bad luck. My father left a defeated man. Owning the land would have been his vindication. There were no signs that the ICA would ever change course. No one could have predicted that the military dictator, Juan Peron, would be the one that freed Jewish farmers from their Jewish oppressor.

My parents and sisters arrived in Buenos Aires, and I still had no passages. I was still working and spending my lunch hours and any bit of other free time chasing the elusive passages. We ended up traveling overnight on a boat to Montevideo from where we took a Pan American flight to New York. That overnight crossing of the turbulent Rio de la Plata in a decrepit boat was a nightmarish experience. The flight took 35 hours including five refueling stops. We did not land in New York where our relatives were gathered to greet us. For some reason that escapes me, the plane was diverted to the Washington, D.C. airport. The New York relatives alerted my mother's sister Anna, who lived in Washington, about this denouement. And so we were met in the middle of the night by three flabbergasted Projectors, Anna, Harry, and their son Theodore. We just had a few moments before we were taken to a train station to board a train to New York. We arrived exhausted at the train station and, without fanfare, were met by two people, Uncle Sam and Aunt Leike.

We had been on the wait-list for nearly 20 years to enter and live in the USA. I was 21 years old and had five years of English in school and an accounting degree. My sister Sonia was 17 and in high school, and our little sister Ines was six. Our parents had been in business from the time they married. They hoped to be able to use their experience. It was a sad and hopeful arrival.

Sonia, Ines and Ann, shortly after arriving in the US 1946

AFTERWORD

In 1994, our mother was severely injured in an automobile accident. During her long recovery, she reflected on how close she had come to dying, and how her grandchildren, three of them then very small, might not have a chance to know her story. Many of her friends had expressed interest in her life and were encouraging her to record it in a memoir. And so, while in the rehabilitation facility she began to write her recollections longhand on yellow legal pads, and thus began a twenty year process of writing this account.

She would write from memory, come to incidents or periods that were unclear and began to communicate with the family, in Argentina, Israel and elsewhere, exploring, discovering and confirming various parts of the story. She moved from paper to word processor, expanded her telephone and email exchanges and circulated drafts in English and Spanish as the story unfolded.

Mother meant this to be the story of her journey to and through Argentina, and that is what it is, ending with the arrival of the family in the United States. Her parents and sisters settled in Brooklyn, N.Y., where her parents ran a candy store with a lunch counter and soda fountain. She lived with a relative in Washington, D.C. where she met our father, Alvin Schorr, and married. They lived for a few years in small towns in Pennsylvania and Ohio, where we were born, before returning to the D.C. area for a dozen years. They lived in New York City for the 1970's and then in Cleveland for 25 years, before moving to a retirement community in Charlotte, N.C., where two of us live.

She had an active career as a computer programmer and statistician, with punch cards and printouts, before keyboards and monitors. She worked first with Defense Department contractors in the DC area programming for war games, then with the New York City Board of Education and the elderly nutrition program in New York City government, and finally directing research with the Cleveland Jewish Federation, before retiring. Throughout her life, she pursued her education in pieces as she could, collecting credits from several colleges and finally obtaining her Bachelor's Degree from New York University in 1973. She had a vibrant and determined volunteer life, participating in voter registration, civil rights, anti-poverty and anti-Vietnam War efforts, and many others.

She described her life as a long journey starting from a relatively affluent and cultured life in Eastern Europe. Her father moved the family away from the oppressive conditions that were developing for Jews in Europe early enough to escape what would become the Holocaust. The only place he could find for them to go, however, was the wilderness of rural Argentina that is described in these memoirs. Years later they arrived in the United States and she eventually attained a life at the very heart of the civilized world in the center of Manhattan.

It is an extraordinary story of courage and persistence, strength and love that saw her own life move from the harsh and austere edge to the lively and vital center of the world, and that gave her children and grandchildren a set of opportunities that would have been unimaginable to her in her youth.

We are acutely aware of and exceptionally grateful to her for the sacrifices she made and the love she shared with us and with all of those who were a part of her journey.

Jessica, Kenneth, and Wendy

32813309R00078

Made in the USA
Lexington, KY
03 June 2014